SPORTS
AND FAITH
Stories of the Devoted
and the Devout

To Father Sean

PATRICK McCASKEY

Pat McCaskey

Sporting Chance Press™, Inc.
1074 Butler Drive
Crystal Lake, IL 60014
sportingchancepress.com

Photographs appearing in *Sports and Faith: Stories of the Devoted and the Devout* were supplied by Mark Bolster, Chaz Palla / *Pittsburgh-Tribune Review,* Cliff Grassmick, the McCaskey family, the University of Colorado, David Bernacchi, the Associated Press, Steve Penland, Tom Connelly/Notre Dame College Prep, *1967 Maridon /*Notre Dame High School Yearbook, Lee Ann Sanderson, Gil Wagle, Wake Forest University, Fordham University, Haymarket Center, the Library of Congress, Wheaton College, and Jonathan Daniel */Lake County News.* Please see the Photographs Credits Table on page 216 for information.

Sports and Faith: Stories of the Devoted and the Devout is Book One of a planned series.

– CONTENTS –

— INTRODUCTION —

The McCaskey family members are caretakers of the Chicago Bears football team. In that capacity, there are many responsibilities. As a sports franchise, we are charged with putting an entertaining and inspiring team on the field. We develop winning programs. We hire and manage professional coaches and administrators who work with us under tremendous pressure to succeed. We strive for excellence for our fans to whom we owe a great debt for supporting us through both good and lean times. Success in sports often runs in cycles and we must keep hope and confidence alive in all we do. We have built today's team on the legacy and example of its founder, George Halas.

Contrary to some opinions, the Bears are not all about business. But the Bears must survive financially from one season to the next to continue the legacy that we have inherited.

Key to all our efforts are our players—our extended family. NFL players often start their careers as young athletes. Their maturity and development as both players and men is a continuing process. These men are modern gladiators, warriors who each week take part in an intense contest that demands great skill and even greater courage.

It's long been said that there are no atheists in foxholes. There are few on the football field. Faith is fundamental to our caretaking efforts. The Bears have a long tradition of working with religious men and women to help our players and staff have continuing spiritual enrichment should they choose it. In this way, the Bears have helped facilitate religious services and support that are often managed by the players themselves. Life is tough and for NFL players, the game carries with it a cadre of additional challenges that most mortals don't face.

I have been blessed to have the opportunity to see, hear, and experience the efforts of the faith community that has grown and nurtured the Bear family for decades. From religious leaders, from devout players and inspired coaches— the faith experience and struggles are part of my DNA.

Also in my capacity of working with charities, I have been blessed to have the opportunity to see and hear exceptional men and women who have devoted much of their lives to faith in action. These incredible people devote themselves to helping those who need help the most. The Bear family's involvement in such charitable efforts is humbling and inspirational.

I have also been blessed with friends and family who have taken the road less traveled outside of sports. They have directed their lives around public service and faith.

As a copious note taker and collector of inspirational experiences, I hope to bring you in on many of the conversations and experiences that have inspired and moved me. These pages recount some of my favorites. Included as well are a bit of inspirational writings and my own small contributions that are often seasoned with a bit of McCaskey humor.

A Bears' Prayer

Bitterness is spiritual cancer.
Forgiveness is spiritual rapture.
Weather is a reminder that God is The Boss.
The Spirit strengthens us, even after a loss.
Jesus Christ is The Man; salvation is the plan.
When we dance God's dance, He gives us another chance.
God's work is efficient; His food is sufficient.
Here's a part of my prayers; bear down, Chicago Bears.

—Patrick McCaskey

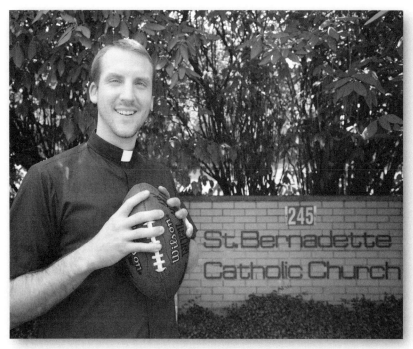

FATHER JOE FREEDY AT SAINT BERNADETTE CHURCH
IN MONROEVILLE, PENNSYLVANIA

HERE I AM

COACH CABRAL WITH COLORADO PLAYERS

We all have to go where God sends us. Each
Christian has a calling; you in your corner;
I in mine. There is a world to be saved.[1]

—Corrie ten Boom

An athlete is a competitor who has abilities to be
developed. Each year, the competitor moves up
to the next level—improving skills and developing physically. And like a singer or an actor, a poet or a
carpenter, the athlete hears the call to follow a dream and
then takes steps to reach it.

These dream chasers are all around us....A young man stays out on the basketball court past dark practicing his jump shot. A teenage tennis player spends endless hours in front of the rebounding board battling an invisible Serena one minute and Venus the next. Back in time, there is the young Dick Butkus, barely old enough for school, spending hours kicking an old football off a tee made from an old Skippy peanut butter jar until his mother calls him in for dinner.[2]

The athlete hears a call to compete, to excel, that is as loud as the dinner bell. The athlete is given a direction in life and is compelled to follow it. Confidence is gained from achievement. Success builds upon success. It is easy for the athlete to believe that it is all about personal achievement and control. "It's all about me."

But many come to understand that God has got their number. Athletic careers are lost in seconds to injury. It's important for the athlete to compete, to be directed toward goals, but it is more important for the athlete to accept who is doing the directing. Everyone needs to surrender to the will of God—to just say, "Here I am Lord; I've come to do your will." It is not an easy lesson.

JOE FREEDY

Almost a decade ago, a Buffalo newspaper's sports headline read: "University of Buffalo Bulls Defeats

Ohio Bobcats 44–0." In that game, Buffalo quarterback Joe Freedy threw for a season-high 296 yards to lead the Bulls to a stunning victory. UB had moved up to Division 1A and wins had been few that season and would be for the next few years. Freedy's offense piled up 538 yards total and life was sweet for the handsome young man who commanded his team. He had good friends, a pretty girlfriend, and a good family. He was loved and respected.

Joe Freedy would go on to graduate the following year after he put up some solid career numbers on the University of Buffalo gridiron. Upon graduation, he had many options. He chose what many would call an unlikely path for a handsome young quarterback—the priesthood.

Joe Freedy had developed an interest in a religious vocation as a young boy. It is a common consideration for untold numbers of boys, but one that often fades in time as manhood approaches. It was not something he talked about much and he had put it on the back burner. His family was a quiet Catholic family—going to Mass, praying at meals, and following the tenets of the faith. Perhaps life was also just a little too busy to notice Joe's interest much with five children running about. Nevertheless, the Freedy parents' faith had spoken volumes to their son. When his mother looked back, she recalled that after all, Joe had been prayerful from an early age. Young Freedy was also influenced by the religious he knew and by what he had read.

Freedy's Lesson

Yet, there were obstacles to his vocation and obstacles that kept Joe from being true to himself. Freedy talks about what drove him as a boy. He remembers being young and wanting to be loved and accepted more than anything else. He remembers going through the motions of being a Christian—going to Mass each week, but thinking that God was boring and burdensome. A "big man on campus" in high school, Freedy had natural athletic abilities that made it easy to compete and excel so he could easily win the adulation of classmates. That adulation seemed to keep him content at least for a while. But once he was in college at the University of Buffalo, everything changed.

At UB, everyone on the field was a gifted athlete. There were no free passes to success. Without a solid work ethic, Freedy found himself so far down the depth chart, it seemed like he had no chance at all to even play in a game. It seemed sports no longer offered him that feeling of being loved and valued as a person. So he turned to other means to become popular. He bought into a new creed that said happiness comes from money, power, pleasure, and fame. He took the path of least resistance. For a short time he bought into the "Animal House" theory of education. He partied hardy, but before long found himself miserable.

Like many other young men who travel down the wrong path, he was pulled back on track by a girl. He met a young woman who exuded an honest dignity and femininity. And in her goodness, he was able to reflect back on her his own sense of masculinity.

Through an odd twist of fate, injuries to other players on UB's football team pushed Freedy into position to play. Responsibility fell quickly on his shoulders and now he faced the challenge to respond and become the committed athlete who would lead his team rather than let it down. He responded and grew in maturity.

Off the field, he took a harder look at his parents and began to get a better appreciation of their faith and character. He saw and understood, perhaps for the first time, a real piety in his father. In his junior year his father gave him a copy of Scot Hahn's *The Lamb's Supper,* which helped him develop a whole new appreciation for his church and helped renew a sense of vocation in him. Hahn's book became Joe Freedy's "playbook" for the priesthood. Its message of enthusiasm for the Eucharist cast a spotlight on the priest's role in bringing that sacrament to Christ's people every day. The book had a powerful influence.

Celibacy and Beyond

As Freedy was drawn again to the vocation of the priesthood, he was torn with having to break away from the young woman who had helped to right him. Their relationship became an on-again, off-again one—heading toward marriage one day, then splitting apart another. After circumstances pulled them geographically apart for a time, his sweetheart found someone else. A period of painful adjustment followed, but was followed by a healing grace.

After college, it was time for Joe to channel his zeal into his vocation and his calling to serve others. "It was a huge tug on my heart," Freedy said, "but the Lord was calling me to this." He had to break from his friends to dedicate himself to preparing for his ministry. He received his master's degree in philosophy from Duquesne University and attended the Pontifical North American College at the Vatican.

Monsignor Sciera of Pittsburgh counseled Freedy on his vocation and when they were both in Rome, the monsignor brought him along to a private chapel in Saint Peter's, where the monsignor said a private Mass alongside the pontiff. Freedy remembered feeling the pope's holiness in a tangible way as John Paul II came into the chapel. The pontiff was ill and it was painful for him to move about, but the Mass was a highly charged faith experience. Afterward, Freedy had a chance to meet John Paul II. Freedy recalled, "I knelt in front of him and hadn't planned on saying anything. I just said, 'I love you,' and he gave me a big smile and his blessing."[3]

While Joe Freedy was studying in Rome, Pope John Paul II died. Freedy was still in Rome for the election of Pope Benedict XVI. Along with thousands of others in Saint Peter's Square, he received Benedict XVI's first papal blessing.

Joe Freedy became Father Joe Freedy when he was ordained in 2008, but his education continued at Pontifical

College. As a priest, he was asked to say Mass for the Missionaries of Charity, the religious order of Mother Teresa that was stationed in Rome. "I celebrated Mass for them once every two weeks," Father Freedy said. "I've been profoundly moved by their love for Jesus and his poor, by the way they serve and give themselves so completely to him, and, most of all, by their joy."

Sister Agnes, the superior in Rome, arranged for Father Freedy to visit their mission in Addis Ababa, Ethiopia. Like Mother Teresa's mission in India, the Sisters in Ethiopia often take the dying from the streets and bring them in to look after them. Father Freedy expressed surprise at what he found at the Sisters' mission just outside of Addis Ababa in Jimma:

> … surprising, to me was the joy and openness of the people, and the courage with which they suffered, …The love with which they related to one another, the sisters and myself often moved me to tears.[4] "Love and peace begin with a smile," Mother Teresa used to say, and this was the way I was always greeted. I would often have to remind myself as I visited and walked around the home, which housed over 300 of Jimma's poor, suffering from HIV, malaria, typhoid, or many other diseases and infections, that these people, these babies, or children, or women and men, are suffering terribly because their faces often betrayed that there was anything wrong.[5]

Never before had I encountered such tremendous suffering, and, at the same time, never before had I seen so dramatically how hope in God can elevate and strengthen the human heart, so that suffering can be transformed into something beautiful for God....Along with being so edified by the poor in my time in Ethiopia, I also learned a tremendous amount from and was formed by the sisters with whom I lived and served while I was there—It is in giving that one receives.

The joy that radiated from these sisters helped me to understand that this is not just a nice maxim, but is the truth of life. They had totally given themselves to Jesus and his thirst to be present to the poorest of the poor. Their joy expressed the gift they had received in return. Their lives are lives of prayer and service, and though they experience human struggles like all of us, they are witnesses in the midst of material poverty that the peace which surpasses all understanding is a gift received from God alone.

After completing his courses at Pontifical North American College in Rome, Father Joe returned to the Pittsburgh Diocese where he has served in parish work. He is currently director of vocations for the Diocese. He is looking to help those other quarterbacks who may receive the special signals outside the huddle that he himself received.

TIM FOLEY

Tim Foley was born January 22, 1948, at St. Vincent's Hospital in Chicago, an institution that served unwed mothers. An adoption had been prearranged. Eight days later, he joined his adoptive parents in Wilmette, Illinois. He attended Saint Francis Xavier Grammar School and Chicago area prep powerhouse, Loyola Academy.

The 1965 Loyola Ramblers lost their first football game to Chicago Saint Rita. The Ramblers won the rest. Tim played quarterback, defense, and kick returner. In the seventh game, he separated his throwing shoulder while running back a kickoff. Billy O'Donnell was the second quarterback; he got hurt in a Chicago Catholic League playoff game. Ken Kracovic was the Ramblers' third quarterback.

When Loyola beat Chicago Saint Leo and Chicago Vocational in the city playoffs, Ken was at the helm. After the season, there weren't many colleges interested in a quarterback with a pin in his shoulder, even though Tim had made the New World All-American Team.

Purdue was the only school to offer Tim a scholarship. The Boilermakers had future pro Mike Phipps to play quarterback. The team had future College Football Hall of Famer Leroy Keyes to break records at running back. Foley adjusted. He played defense. He started three years at cornerback and set punt return records. He was an All-American.

Tim's life goal was to play in the College All-Star game. He broke his ankle at a Fellowship of Christian Athletes (FCA) conference in June 1970. He did not play in the All-Star Game. Undeterred, he got to the Miami Dolphins training camp early as a third-round draft choice. He started as a rookie and ran back kicks. He played cornerback for seven seasons under Coach Don Shula. Tim tore a knee in 1976. He adjusted again. He switched to safety and made All-Pro. He tore his other knee in 1980 and that ended his football-playing career.

Here I Am, Lord

The Good Lord had Tim's number and he came to know it. Fellow players respected Tim and he was in charge of chapel service for the Dolphins. According to Tim,

> You need faith in tough times. Struggles bring us to our knees and make us better and add depth to our lives. When bad things happen, think: what's the lesson? This is happening to you because you need the work. For every 100 people who can deal with adversity, only one can handle success.

Tim spoke to the Bears as chapel speaker before a game with the Dolphins:

> I survived in the NFL on emotion. To me you're just a bunch of guys who have insecurities like

everyone else. I want to talk about Jesus. Your faith can make you a better athlete. All my life I've never enjoyed sports until 1976, when I had a knee injury and switched to safety. I made up my mind to enjoy it as much as possible.

We are examples to our teammates in how we act. Do we make them feel that they are better than us? You should be aware of other people's needs. You are servants. It's an orientation toward others that Jesus had. It's a feeling of warmth and compassion that Jesus had. After time with Jesus, some apostles asked who is the most important. They were missing the point.

You have been saved not only for the next life, but also for this one. Faith is for now. Faith is to remove jealousy and greed from my heart. As a defensive back, humility is a play away. My life has been directed. Every time I tried to go away from God, that door was shut.

David, Solomon, and all the prophets had problems. God is trying to teach you something with trials. You want your children to know that beyond everything, you love them. God is like that with us. We have to be that way with our teammates. As soon as you can in your athletic career, have a good time. Enjoy it. It's a short time of your life.

BRIAN CABRAL

In general, for every player who sees a lot of action in an NFL game, there is another one who spends most of his time on the bench. It is not easy for a player who has competed at the highest level in each age group to be inactive during a game.

During Brian Cabral's six-year Chicago Bear career, he started eight games. He and Steve Parolini have chronicled Brian's "struggle with self-esteem and the meaning of success" in a book for young adults (ages 12 and up) entitled *Second String Champion*.[6] Things never quite worked out the way Brian would have liked them to in football.

Brian had high expectations. His father was the first Hawaiian to play football for the University of Notre Dame. He wanted to be the second. When he was in high school, Brian got up at six and took two buses to school. He did not get home from football practice until eight o'clock. His coach made sure the team went to Mass before every game. When colleges recruited him, Brian told them that he wanted to play for Notre Dame. After Notre Dame rejected him, he played for Bill Mallory at the University of Colorado.

At Colorado, Brian got married during his junior year. The coaches did not like the idea, so Brian lived in the player dorms during senior year training camp to demonstrate his commitment to the program. Marriage to Becky helped make him a better player.

When he was a junior at Colorado, Brian heard all-pro Cleveland Browns defensive end Bill Glass talk about playing football to honor God. Then Brian started to read the Bible and learn from other people who talked about their faith.

The Atlanta Falcons drafted Brian in the fourth round of the 1978 NFL draft. Before he left for rookie training camp with the Falcons, he went to a Fellowship of Christian Athletes conference. He developed a better relationship with God and it gave Brian a sense of peace. After the Falcons, Brian played for the Baltimore Colts, the Green Bay Packers, and the Chicago Bears. He recalled his Bear days:

> My role shifted a bit from year to year. But after playing alongside Mike Singletary in my first year and backing up the outside linebacker in my second, Buddy Ryan moved me to back up Mike Singletary in the middle linebacker position. "On the field, I was Mike's backup. I knew I wouldn't start unless Mike couldn't. My new role had been established.
>
> One of the greatest witnesses we can have as Christians is our intensity. Whenever I read Colossians 3:23, "Whatever you do, work at it with all your heart, as working for the Lord, not for men," I see a challenge to Christians to be intense—to strive for excellence.

Mike Singeltary and I started to grow closer when I was his backup with the Bears. We became roommates and I encouraged him to attend our fellowship group. Over time, we developed a friendship that transcended our roles on the football field.

If you strive for a goal and the goal continues to elude you, it might be time to change direction. But before you change direction, you may have to change your attitude.

Pride is the first thing you'll need to deal with. A large part of the competitive nature is pride. I wanted to play; I wanted to start. Although I never would admit it, my pride in playing football ran deep. Swallowing my pride meant redirecting my desires to match the Lord's plans for me.

Because Cabral couldn't beat out Singletary as the starting middle linebacker, Brian tried to help the team in other ways. He led the special teams in tackles and became captain of those units. He also organized the team Bible studies and arranged for the chapel speakers before the games. Brian's teammates knew about his faith. He did not try to hide it. He was intense and forthright. He did not isolate himself from those who did not attend the Bible studies. He went to team parties and to the town pub after training camp evening meetings. He drank sodas and played darts and pool.

On those occasions, Brian did not initiate discussions about faith. His teammates did. He built bridges with the Bible. He did not use it as a weapon; he was honest about his faith and with his teammates. Some of them appreciated his invitations to the team Bible studies. Some of them did not. He learned through both reactions. He kept growing and learning about what success in God's eyes meant.

Brian occasionally substituted for Mike Singletary as the Bears middle linebacker. Mike replaced Brian as the Bears spiritual leader. Singletary wrote about the impact that Cabral made on him and the Bears. Thanks to Brian, Mike's goal has been to be the best Christian, the best husband, and the best father he can be.

Brian wanted to retire from playing while he was still healthy and he wanted to leave on good terms with the club. He noticed that very few players did. When it was time to leave, Brian talked with Bears head coach Mike Ditka and Bears president Mike McCaskey. They expressed their appreciation for the good job that he did. He left on a good note.

Brian has coached football at the University of Colorado for over 20 years in several capacities. The change in his college plans from Notre Dame to Colorado would work out to his benefit in many ways. Considered one of the best developers of linebackers in the country, he has also been instrumental in scouting, recruiting, and mentoring Hawaiian and other Polynesian players.

Brian continues to develop his relationship with Jesus—attending a church that keeps him grounded, seeking fellowship of other believers, and looking out for those who can encourage his faith and counsel him.

BILL WADE

Bill Wade was born on October 4, 1930, at Vanderbilt Hospital. His father, William Wade Sr., was captain of the Vanderbilt football team in 1921 and Bill followed in his footsteps. He received a scholarship from Coach Red Sanders and became a fine quarterback. While the Commodore Team had modest success during his years there, he set school passing records, and was selected SEC Player of the year in 1951.[7]

Drafted by the Los Angeles Rams as their first pick in the 1951 draft, he served as a Naval officer for two years before he joined the team. After seven years with the Rams, Wade joined the Bears in 1961 and stayed through 1966. Chicago Bears Hall of Famer Doug Atkins described Wade's toughness: "He could run the ball and when he ran the ball, he never slid. He'd try and run over you. And he did."[8]

In 1963, Wade would lead a talented Bears team to the league championship, but beating the Packers was the number one priority of the team that year. The Bears coaching staff created plays for the Packer matchups before the season began, practiced those plays in training camp, and then sat on them during the season until meeting the Packers. Although Wade's record was not stellar against the Packers overall, he led the Bears to two critical victories in 1963. Wade would recall his games against Green Bay: "…I feel at peace when I remember these contests. There is something honorable about giving your all and that was always what happened when these two teams meet."[9]

On Sunday, December 29, 1963, the Bears played the New York Giants at Wrigley for the Championship. In the first quarter, Bill Wade had a two-yard touchdown run. In the third quarter, Wade had a one-yard touchdown run. The Bears won 14–10.

When I was seven, I started going to Bears training camps with Papa Bear George Halas. Bill Wade taught us how to play quarterback. After the Bears' two-a-day practices, Bill Wade tutored me in the fundamentals of quarterbacking. Before each session with me, he would reach down to the ground and find a four-leaf clover. That meant we would have a good workout. He also said, "Everyone I've ever tutored in quarterbacking became an All-American." That was a confidence builder. Bill was an excellent teacher.

Bill served in a coaching capacity at the end of his career with the Bears. George Halas wanted to retain him, but Wade decided to retire and go home to spend more time with his family.

BILL WADE PASSING WITH BOB WETOSKA PROTECTING

Wade's Faith

In 1962, the American Tract Society published Bill's tract, "Quarterback for Christ,"[10] in which he wrote:

> When sportswriters and others ask me for my greatest thrill, they no doubt have in mind some dramatic game or specific play that occurred during my collegiate years at Vanderbilt University, my seven years with the Los Angeles Rams, or my experience with the Chicago Bears. They are usually surprised at my reply.

> First of all, my most thrilling moment in football is yet to come. In the game of life, however, my most thrilling moment to date would have to be the decision I made after Navy officer Jim Wilson talked to me for about six hours back in 1953. Though I had been brought up in a Christian home, with wonderfully devout parents, Jim impressed upon me the necessity for a personal surrender to Jesus Christ as Saviour and Lord. A new aim and purpose in my life resulted from my spiritual transaction at that time.

> In the game of pro football, there are many injuries which could be avoided. The best way to avoid these injuries, in my opinion, is to keep your body physically fit.

When we consider life, whether it be for 10 years or 100, we are participating in a series of games. We will readily admit that the game of life is basically spiritual. As we play the game and learn our purpose, whether it be president of a bank, worker in a factory, secretary, or quarterback of a football team, we must exercise ourselves spiritually to win the daily battles of life.

I have found there are three basic exercises which strengthen me spiritually. The first is the exercise of prayer. The second is that of reading the Bible. The third is one that is vital to every Christian—that of asking in prayer each day that you might be allowed to talk to someone about the Christian way of life.

If you believe that God has created you, it becomes a supplemental belief that He has created you for a purpose. What purpose? This is answered when we submit ourselves to Him, that His will might be done in our lives.

In talking to youth groups from time to time on the subject of "What It Takes to Play Football," I like to use this acrostic:

C—*Confidence.* "If God be for us, who can be against us?" (Romans 8:31).

H—*Humility.* "He that humbleth himself shall be exalted" (Luke 14:11).

R—*Respect.* We must have a respect of laws, of doing what is right. A healthy respect of others is vital to a fruitful Christian life.

I—*Intelligence.* As a quarterback, one must learn and know a great many things. To be good, useful Christians, we should be as intelligent as possible. "If any of you lack wisdom, let him ask of God, who giveth to all men liberally, and upbraideth not" (James 1:5).

S—*Sincerity.* You must be sincere before people will believe you.

T—*Truth.* "Unto thine own self be true." Don't lie to yourself. Don't try to fool yourself by fooling others.

Many times I have seen a comparatively small 175-pounder tackle a 245-pound fullback successfully. That takes courage. In life itself, there are going to be times when we are called upon to tackle big problems. If we belong to Christ, He gives us the courage to face them.

We can only belong to Him by opening our hearts, allowing Him to cleanse us from our sin, and personally accepting Him as Saviour and Lord of our life.

"If any man be in Christ, he is a new creature: old things are passed away; behold, all things are become new" (2 Corinthians 5:17).

McCaskey's Scout Calling

As a young man, I was called to be a Boy Scout. I was in Saint Mary's Boy Scout Troop 22 in Des Plaines, Illinois. Joe Stucker was the Scoutmaster from 1958 through 1966. Meetings were held in the old school hall on Thursday evenings at 7:30 p.m. We played tackle pom-pom[11] before the meetings started. When Mr. Stucker's hand went up in the three-fingered Scout salute, the mouths were to be shut. That was the theory.

The adult leaders were very dedicated and knowledgeable. Mr. Gilbert, Mr. Littwin, and Mr. Whelan were active adult leaders during Mr. Stucker's reign. The Scouts were a lot of fun and a great peer group. There were overnight outings at Camp Baden Powell and retreats at Villa Redeemer.

On Friday, July 27, 1962, I wrote this letter from Camp Napowan to my parents, Ed & Virginia McCaskey.

Dear Mom and Dad,

Get set for a shock. We had the Order of the Arrow election and I made it. We, John Hannon, Andy Stucker, and I had to sleep in a barn that night after the tap-out ceremony. We would have had to sleep under the stars but it was pouring rain at the time. The next morning we had to find our way back to the Mess Hall by ourselves to get our instructions. Our instructions were Number One: no talking all day except for two question-and-answer periods. Number Two: only bread and milk all day. Number Three: We would work more than we ever did in one day in our whole life. The work we had to do was cut down about ten huge box cedar trees and clear that area for storage. Of course we didn't do it all by ourselves. We had help from candidates from other units and Mr. Whalen also got tapped out. We had nothing but a couple slices of bread and a little milk all day until the banquet at about 10 o'clock that night after the closing ceremony where we received our sashes.

I'm working on about five different merit badges: Lifesaving, Nature, Leatherwork, Cooking, and Camping. I'm Senior Patrol Leader for the last five days for our troop.

Could you please send up the latest major league standings?

Your loving son,

Pat

Now that I am a man, I notice that many scouts have these following characteristics:

1. *A Scout Is Trustworthy*

A Scout's honor is paramount. If he were to violate his honor by giving incomplete reports, or by cheating on his expense account, or by not going to Indianapolis in February for the Combine, he may be directed to turn in his decoder ring.

2. *A Scout Is Loyal*

He is loyal to all to whom loyalty is due: God, his family, his team, his general manager, his secretary, his hometown, his alma maters, his city, his state, his country, his hemisphere, his planet, and his universe.

3. *A Scout Is Helpful*

He must be prepared at any time to workout free agents, help injured players, and search the waiver wires. He is utterly alone except inasmuch as he helps his team.

4. *A Scout Is Friendly*

He is a friend of the earth and a brother to every other Scout. Early in his career, he earns the car rental merit badge. His favorite song is "On the Road Again."

5. A Scout Is Courteous

He is polite to all, especially management, coaches, and players.

6. A Scout Is Kind

He is a friend to animals. The Bears are his favorite team. He displays sportsmanship toward the Bills, Colts, Dolphins, Bengals, Broncos, Seahawks, Cardinals, Eagles, Lions, Falcons, Rams, Ravens, Jaguars, and Panthers. He is also kind to Patriots, Jets, Browns, Titans, Steelers, Chiefs, Raiders, Chargers, Cowboys, Giants, Redskins, Packers, Vikings, Buccaneers, Saints, 49ers, and Texans.

7. A Scout Is Obedient

He obeys the Ten Commandments, his general manager, and his own Scout Law. He obeys the law of gravity because he knows it's there for his protection. He even obeys the speed limit because he doesn't want to forfeit his car rental merit badge.

8. A Scout is Cheerful

He tries to smile all the time, even on draft day. If his choice is not his team's choice, he doesn't stomp out of the draft room in a huff. He follows the philosophy of Mel Brooks as the 2,000-year-old man. "Keep a smile on your face and a nectarine in your pocket."

9. *A Scout Is Thrifty*

He flies coach. If someone accuses him of being cheap, he explains that he always admired Jack Benny. He tithes 10% of his income. He pays his bills promptly. He files his income tax returns on time.

10. *A Scout Is Brave*

He has the courage to speak up for his choices on draft day against the coaxings of other Scouts or the leers or threats of the general manager, and defeat does not discourage him. If his team is in a losing streak because of a lot of injuries, he is prepared to offer suggestions about carefully researched projects on the practice squads of other teams.

11. *A Scout Is Clean*

He cleans up the sink after he is through using it so the next person who uses it won't feel so badly. He does not use obscenities because swear words are clichés. He knows the importance of keeping himself physically fit. He knows it's even more important to shower after his workouts.

12. *A Scout Is Reverent*

He has a mature love of God. He longs for the attainment of the full capacity to love. He goes to church or mosque or temple and has daily devotions. If he scouts a player who will be great and who has different religious convictions, he still recommends the player.

— ENDNOTES —

[1] Ten Boom, Corrie, *Not I, But Christ* (Nashville, TN: Thomas Nelson, 1983), 47.

[2] Dick Butkus and Pat Smith, *Butkus Flesh and Blood* (New York: Doubleday, 1997), 2.

[3] Tim Graham, "Signal Calling—UB Quarterback Foregoes Family and Career to Train for Priesthood in Rome," July 3, 2005, *Buffalo News*, viewed at: http://www.freerepublic.com/focus/religion/1436452/posts?page=1 (accessed October 27, 2010).

[4] Chuck Moody, "Joy and Openness Amid the Poorest in Ethiopia," February 9, 2009, *Pittsburgh Catholic*, viewed at http://www.pittsburghcatholic.org/newsarticles_more.phtml?id=2403 (accessed October 27, 2010).

[5] Moody, "Joy and Openness Amid the Poorest in Ethiopia."

[6] Cabral, Brian, *Second String Champion* (Loveland, CO: Group Publishing (Teenage Books), 1990), 71-75. Quotes used with permission of the author.

[7] Richard Scott, *SEC Football: 75 Years of Pride and Passion*, (Minneapolis, MN: MBI Publishing Company (Voyageur Press), 2008), 100.

[8] Scott, *SEC Football: 75 Years of Pride and Passion*, 100.

[9] Beth Gorr, *Bear Memories: The Chicago-Green Bay Rivalry* (Mount Pleasant, SC, Arcadia Publishing, 2005), 45-46.

[10] Bill Wade, "Quarterback for Christ" (Garland, TX: American Tract Society, 1962). Used by permission of American Tract Society, PO Box 462008, Garland, TX 75046-2008, www.ATStracts.org. 800–548–7228.

[11] Perhaps the best game ever devised to keep children in shape. It is also known as Black Peter, wall to wall, and pom pom pullaway. In this tag game a chaser seeks to tag (or tackle) players as they run from one safety zone to the other. Each tagged person becomes a chaser and the game continues until everyone is tagged. The first person tagged becomes the original chaser in the next game. The chaser signals the beginning of each run from zone to zone by calling out "pom pom."

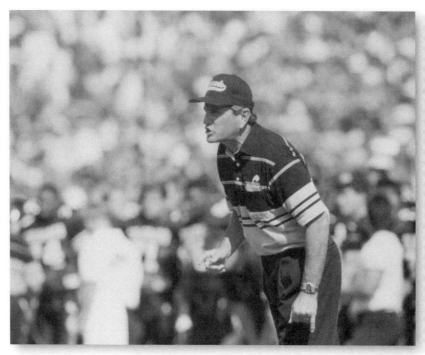

BILL McCARTNEY INSTRUCTING

TAKES THE BROKEN

A FIELD OF SPORTS AND FAITH

Athletes, like everyone else, are not perfect on or off the field. It takes training and practice to achieve good results in sports. It takes extraordinary dedication to achieve excellence.

We can become obsessed with our games and our athletes. Sports are important to us. We put our sports heroes on pedestals, although we are warned that they are just human beings. The media chronicles the continuing slips and falls of our heroes. Some fans become cynical. Others learn to cheer with the victories and suffer the defeats graciously.

Regardless of the outcomes, there are always lessons to be learned. Stories of people who overcome their defeats are inspiring.

BILL MCCARTNEY

Bill McCartney was born in Detroit on August *22,* 1940. He earned 11 letters in football, basketball, and baseball at Riverview High School. He went to the University of Missouri on a football scholarship. He was a three-year letterman.

McCartney met his wife through a mutual friend. She said, "Hey Mac, you want to get married?" He replied, "How about we dance first?" They dated for a year and got married while they were still in college.

After he had graduated, McCartney coached football and basketball at high schools in Missouri and Michigan. While he was at Divine Child High in Dearborn, Michigan, the football and basketball teams won the state championship in the same school year. Later in his career, McCartney became an assistant football coach at the University of Michigan. Legendary head coach Bo Schembechler said, "Bill's the kind of guy who's so forthcoming that if you ask him for the time of day, he'll tell you how to make a watch."

Pinnacle of Success in Football

McCartney was 93–55–5 at the University of Colorado. Under Coach McCartney, the Buffalos won three Big Eight titles and notched their first national championship in 1990. They played in nine bowl games.[1]

During the 1994 season, the Buffalos managed a win at the University of Michigan that is known as the "Miracle in Michigan." The play is perhaps as famous for Buffalo fans as Franco Harris's "Immaculate Reception" is for Steeler fans. In a tight match played in Ann Arbor on September 24, 1994, the Buffalos were trailing the Wolverines 26–21 with six seconds left in the game. Buffalo quarterback, Kordell Stewart, threw a 70-yard bomb into the end zone that Michael Westbrook snagged off a deflection by Blake Anderson. McCartney called the play himself and it must have been a sweet win for him as the former assistant coach of the Wolverines.

McCartney had risen to the pinnacle of college football success, but the effort had taken a toll on him and his family. In early 1995, four years after winning the national championship, the Buffalos finished another successful season by beating Notre Dame in the Fiesta Bowl.

In both the AP and the Coaches polls, the Buffalos were ranked number three for the season. Yet, in the midst of becoming one of the most sought-after coaches in the sport to which he had devoted much of his life, Bill McCartney called it quits. It was time to devote himself fully to God and his family. He had always taken the position that family should take precedence over football and it had become impossible to manage his priorities at that time while coaching.

McCartney at Home

McCartney is a devout Christian and his family faced tough times. McCartney's retirement from coaching allowed him to focus on his family—his daughter, three sons, and grandchildren who would need him. But more than anything else, Bill McCartney believed he needed to give his wife, Lyndi, the companionship and support she deserved and had simply never gotten while he was a coach.

McCartney and Lyndi root for their athletic grandchildren. Timothy J. (T. J.) McCartney was trained as a quarterback by two McCartney coaches—informally by his grandfather Bill McCartney and, officially, by his uncle Tom McCartney who coached him at Fairfiew High. LSU called TJ's number. The offensive and defensive end position is where grandson Derek McCartney has seen action in high school.

God Takes the Broken

McCartney and Dave Diles wrote a book, *From Ashes To Glory,* published by Thomas Nelson.[2] In the Introduction, McCartney wrote:

When the question of my getting the job as head football coach at the University of Colorado was still unsettled, I made it clear to those doing the hiring that football was not the number one priority in my life. I explained that it was God first, family second, and football third.

And nothing has changed.

I have no problem with exposing myself to the world for what I really am. I'm an ordinary guy with an extraordinary God. I want to share with everyone the struggles I have been through, struggles that reinforced rather than sapped my belief that God is faithful. There is no hesitation about telling the truth, no apprehension about sharing my fears and my doubts.

I am not afraid to tell the world that I have a struggle with alcohol; that I have a battle with my temper; that I agonize over things that are said and written about me and my family; that I second-guess myself a lot, that I ponder whether I am worthy; that I have feelings of guilt.

If someone says, "Oh, another Jesus freak, here we go again!" I'll understand. I am not ashamed of the Gospel of Jesus Christ. I don't want to cram my beliefs down anybody's throat, but I must proclaim my faith. If I do not proclaim Christ before men, He won't proclaim me before His Father in Heaven. I must not be intimidated lest I offend someone, else I wouldn't be God's man.

McCartney prays so that he can give his squad "the leadership required to turn them into a team, instead of merely a group of talented individuals." When there was a family problem, the McCartneys:

> ...Understood that among all the promises of God, there is not one that suggests life will be easy. It is not written that following Jesus Christ will eliminate every problem. We had no right to expect a trouble-free existence, and we accepted that.

> I think it is difficult for the best of us, in times of great crisis or stress, to maintain that peace that passes all understanding. And I'm convinced that we are not always immediately reinforced by the Scripture that reminds us to pray "...not as I will, but as thou wilt."

> The Psalms gave me comfort when I couldn't quite muster the level of trust I knew God wanted me to place in Him. David, after all, had made his share of mistakes, too...But God sent a prophet to David, and David confessed his sins. And God is great on

forgiveness. He cleansed David of all unrighteous-
ness, and David is the only man in the Bible who is
described as a man after God's own heart.

For everyone in our family, there was the terrible
temptation to lash out....We tried to stay close to
each other and to God....Every member of our
family knew that only with God's help would we
face our tomorrows with any kind of hope that this,
too, would pass.

After leaving the University of Colorado, Bill Mc-
Cartney founded the Promise Keepers, a Christian
Men's organization. He left the Promise Keepers when
his wife became ill in 2003, but has recently returned
to the organization.

ROD GRAVES

Rod Graves is a former football scout who worked his way
up to general manager of the Arizona Cardinals. Before
moving to the Cardinals, he was Chicago Bears director of
player personnel. His father, Jackie Graves, was similarly
employed by the Philadelphia Eagles. While with the Bears,
Rod spoke about his experiences in facing life's challenges.
    Rod spoke about the problems that we may encoun-
ter with others—especially those who are very close to us.
If we want to try to change other people, to fix everyone

else, life can get frustrating. Problems became insurmountable for Rod when he put everything on his shoulders.

> "At this particular juncture, I decided to give up on
> doing things myself and to put it all in the hands of
> God. I decided to concentrate heavily on myself
> and leave the rest to God. At that point, I began to
> pray quite a bit…to stop trying to rectify our prob-
> lems with my own power."

Speaks Forgiveness

Rod learned a great deal from the Bible's account of Joseph:

> As I think about that problem and I really just put it
> all in a capsule, I think a lot about Joseph in Genesis
> when he was sold into slavery by his brothers. His
> brothers didn't really care for him. They envied Jo-
> seph because he had been born to Jacob and Joseph
> was his favorite son. His brothers really resented all
> of the attention he received from his father.
>
> So they decided to trap him. They decided to kill
> him. In retrospect, they decided that wouldn't be
> a good thing to do, but they sold him into slavery.
> Through an occurrence of events, Joseph went
> from slavery all the way to the most powerful man
> in Egypt. When he visited with his brothers one

afternoon, Joseph's response to them was basically, "I forgive you for everything that you've done. I have no animosity. I have no vengeance toward you."

Joseph took a different perspective. He said to his brothers, "Because you sold me into slavery, God had a different purpose for my life that neither you nor I could understand." Because, through his involvement in Egypt, he was able to save lives from the famine. Joseph took a different approach to his brothers. He had a feeling of love and compassion with his brothers once he viewed them again.

I tell that story because it shows us that we can take a different approach to the way we view problems and the way that we view any troubles that we have in our lives. By just being faithful to God, by prayer, and through faith and prayer, God will continue to work in our lives.

If there are any of you out there tonight who are struggling with problems, faith and prayer are the only way I would suggest to really meet your problems head on and to get you beyond that point where you feel like nothing is going to happen on your own power.

So I suggest tonight that faith and prayer is the way to go. Even though football is a violent and very tough game, we depend a great deal on God's help to get us through. I just wanted to pass that message on because it's something that all of us can use daily in our lives. Faith, prayer, and being willing to turn over our problems to God to see us through."

FATHER NEVINS

Don Nevins was born in Bloomington, Illinois on February 26, 1949. For Christmas, 1950, he moved with his parents to 434 Thacker Street in Des Plaines, Illinois. He went to West School for kindergarten and Saint Mary's School for grades one to eight. He was a Cub Scout, a Boy Scout, and an altar boy. He played sixth grade football at West Park.

During the second semester of sixth grade, he came down with rheumatic fever. With this condition, a heart murmur usually affects a joint. For Don, it was behind the knees, especially the right. It was difficult to walk. He had complete rest in bed, and he was flat on his back. He didn't feel sick, but he was. When Don got a little better, he played whiffle ball in a wheelchair. He kept up his schoolwork. His sister Fran picked up his assignments. His mother went over everything with him. Sister Irma also came to the house a couple of times. Doctor Conley came from Park Ridge every week to give Don a shot of penicillin in the rear.

God Makes Us Whole

Saint Mary's pastor, Father Bird, came every week and gave Don Holy Communion. That really impressed Don. About the second or third week of seventh grade, Don joined Sister Vitalis's class. He made the baseball team the following spring. He played Little League baseball in the summer. He was captain of the patrol boys in eighth grade. He played on the eighth grade basketball and baseball teams. He played Pony League baseball in the summer.

Don went to Quigley Seminary in Chicago. Teachers would tell him what it was like to be a priest. He completed four years of Latin and English, two of German, and one of Greek. He was president of the junior class. He played shortstop for Quigley in Lincoln Park. He played three seasons of baseball—shortstop and first base. During the summers, he did landscaping and built tennis courts. He was learning Spanish at the time because he worked with Spanish crews.

He also went with other Quigley students to do English and math tutoring in Chicago's Cabrini-Green housing project on Wednesday nights. The television show "Sixty Minutes" called Cabrini-Green "the nation's most infamous public housing project, synonymous with gangs, drugs, misery and murder."

Bus service from the projects was limited and he had to walk several miles to where he boarded at Niles College Seminary of Loyola University. He was also active in the home visitation program in the Austin neighborhood of Chicago that encouraged people to stay in the community to keep it integrated. In his senior year, Don studied in Vienna. His visit stirred his interest in the period between the two world wars. As a history major, he was particularly interested in the late 19th and 20th century American history.

In the fall of 1971, Don enrolled at Saint Mary of the Lake Seminary in Mundelein, Illinois. The students were involved in parish activities in addition to their academics. Don was at Saint Ann's at 18th Place and Leavitt in Chicago on Fridays, and he grew more involved with the priestly life. The Hispanic population in the archdiocese was increasing. Don started studying Spanish at Saint Mary of the Lake.

In the summer of 1973, he went to Cuernavaca, Mexico for intensive language programs. At that time, the Archdiocese of Chicago staffed a mission in Panama. Don stayed there for three weeks. At the end of his third year, he was a deacon at Saint John Fisher at 103rd and Washtenaw in Chicago. He was there from June 1974 until his ordination in May 1975. Don was ordained at his parents' parish, Saint Cecilia, in Mount Prospect, a Chicago suburb. Then he was assigned back to Saint Ann's. One day during the summer of 1980, the tower of the church fell on the rectory just 15 minutes after Don had left his room.

In July 1981, Don returned to Niles College, where he taught theology his first year. In the spring of 1982, he began coaching the baseball team. That summer, he studied Spanish in Spain. The next summer, he studied Spanish in Mexico while the World Cup soccer matches took place. In the summer of 1984, he studied Spanish in Peru. He followed the Cubs division title march on Armed Forces Radio broadcasts late at night.

Don coached the Niles College baseball teams for six years. Some of the students on the team had never played organized ball before, but they developed their skills under Don. After he earned a masters degree in Spanish, he was made the academic dean of the college. His responsibilities increased. On Saturdays there were often doubleheaders and he would say the Spanish Mass at 6:45 p.m. at Saint Mary's in Des Plaines. He loved coaching, but he had to give it up.

On the Wednesday after Easter in 1989, Cardinal Bernardin told Don he would be assigned to Saint Procopius Church in the Pilsen neighborhood of Chicago, where there is a large Spanish-speaking population. The cardinal thought it was time for Don to move on. Don had mixed emotions about it. Don asked himself, where does the diocese have a need? Rather than, where do I want to go? He enjoyed his work at Niles College, but he realized the cardinal was right to send him to Pilsen.

Don was installed as pastor at Saint Procopius on October 1, 1989. In his homily, he said:

Some of my family and friends and students do not understand Spanish. So I'll do the homily again in English. The gospel is about the rich man and Lazarus. The rich man is condemned, not because he is rich, but because he is unwilling to help his brother Lazarus.

The story of Lazarus is one that encourages us to act to help those less fortunate. It was also a poignant way for Don to explain his calling to the Hispanic community:

It is very easy to focus on poverty. We also see a lack of education and gangs. [But] there is a richness here, too. People are willing to help other people. The previous pastor, Father O'Keefe, was able to draw on many leaders in the community. So as I begin my life here, I see poverty, but there is also a richness. Be willing to work together and to share in the solving of the problems.

My boyhood friend Don Nevins is a scholar, an athlete, and a respected voice in the Chicago community. As a young boy, he was broken once, but was made whole again. During his long ministry, he has worked in several Hispanic parishes in Chicago, where he continues to serve.

— ENDNOTES —

[1] Colorado Buffaloes—Official Home of Colorado Athletics, "Bill Mc-Cartney, Football Coach," http://www.cubuffs.com/ViewArticle.dbml?DB_OEM_ID=600&ATCLID=608619, (accessed October 27, 2010).

[2] Bill McCartney and David L. Diles, *From Ashes To Glory* (Nashville, TN, Thomas Nelson Inc., 1995). McCartney quotes are reprinted by permission from *From Ashes To Glory*, Bill McCartney and David L. Diles, copyright 1995, Thomas Nelson Inc. Nashville, Tennessee. All rights reserved.

STEELERS' SUPER BOWL IX PRAYER

THERE IS HOPE

BYRON "WHIZZER" WHITE

Consult not your fears but your hopes and dreams.
Think not about your frustrations, but about your
unfulfilled potential. Concern yourself not with
what you tried and failed in, but with what is still
possible for you to do.

—Pope John XXIII

Hope sustains and encourages us. In many ways it is the virtue of those who lead exemplary lives—those who are active not passive.

Athletes face many tribulations and setbacks in their pursuit of excellence. They must overcome each setback that comes along and maintain hope for the future. Sports can teach us patience, perseverance, and more. But hope is needed in all things we do.

Truly exemplary individuals give hope to the team. Their dedication drives enthusiasm. Enthusiasm is contagious. Often a team that does not have the right "chemistry" is hopeless. A team that is enthusiastic is hopeful.

In football you see the quarterback whose team is behind by three touchdowns with a minute left to go, playing a no huddle offense to get one last touchdown before the gun sounds. There is the determined baseball hitter who steps up to the plate with two outs in the bottom of the ninth, his team behind by 6 runs. He digs in his heels in the batter's box and goes toe-to-toe with the 95-mph fastball like his life depends upon it. In sports, these hopeful athletes help the team every day—in good, bad, and desperate situations.

Outside of sports there are those who maintain hope for others. These people take their hope and transfer it to the most needy, the most troubled, and the most ignored. In them, hope flows through their veins into our brutal streets, our dark alleys, and our hard hearts.

> The virtue of hope responds to the aspiration to happiness which God has placed in the heart of every man; it takes up the hopes that inspire men's activities and purifies them so as to order them to the Kingdom of heaven; it keeps man from

discouragement; it sustains him during times of abandonment; it opens up his heart in expectation of eternal beatitude. Buoyed up by hope, he is preserved from selfishness and led to the happiness that flows from charity.

—Catechism of the Catholic Church[1]

ART ROONEY, THE STEELERS, AND HOPE

Art Rooney was a man with hope. It took 42 years for Art's Steelers to win their first championship. He never lost hope.

Art was raised in an apartment over his father's tavern on the North side of Pittsburgh in an area where Three Rivers Stadium was built. His father had to contend with a thirsty and pugnacious bunch of Irishmen, but he was up to the task. The Rooney boys would grow up tough as well—so tough that they often fought the professional boxers who would come to town with the carnival. The pros who challenged all comers for a purse would eventually challenge all comers except the Rooneys.[2]

Art himself was so good with his fists that he won the AAU welterweight title. He declined an Olympic invitation, although he was probably the best in his weight class. Twice he beat Sammy Mosberg, the man who took Rooney's "spot" on the team—once before the Olympics and once after. Incredibly, Mosberg won gold in the Olympics.[3]

And yet, according to Rooney's son Dan, his father acknowledged that Art's brother Dan Rooney "had more knockouts than Jack Dempsey and most of them were out of the ring." Dan would later become a very tough priest.[4]

The entrepreneurial young Rooney had no taste for work in the steel mills. He followed his own interests. He entered politics and worked as ward manager of the 22nd Ward. He founded and played on the Hope-Harveys, a regional semipro football team. He played baseball at Indiana University of Pennsylvania and later played and managed the Stogies, a minor league team from Wheeling, West Virginia. He signed with the Red Sox, but found he could make more money barnstorming with semipro teams. It was fun and lucrative. He did it for several years. He remained a huge baseball fan his entire life.

He promoted fights and other events—building his wealth in a cornucopia of sports activities. Even when Art became a professional football owner, he continued to maintain many sports interests and businesses. In fact it would be years into his ownership before he came to see professional football with the same zeal as George Halas and some of the other owners—if in fact he ever did. Rooney was a sport Renaissance man.

Professional Football Comes to Rooney

Art Rooney was one of the pillars of the professional football community from its early years. Professional football began in 1920, but the sport struggled to succeed in its early years. Of the original 11 teams, only George Halas's Decatur Staleys and the Racine Cardinals would make it. Teams that dropped out were often replaced by teams that would quickly fail thereafter. A few years into the Depression, Football commissioner Joe F. Carr began to recruit ownership from larger cities. Art Rooney was already a successful sports promoter. Carr approached him about bringing a new team into professional football for a $2,500 entry fee. Young Rooney was not shy about risking the money. Like William Wrigley, who was motivated out of civic pride to bring Chicago a winner when he bought the Cubs, Rooney had civic pride in Pittsburgh and wanted to start a professional team at home. His Pittsburgh club joined the fledgling professional football league on July 8, 1933. Rooney named his team the Pirates, mimicking the baseball franchise, but changed the name to the Steelers in 1940.

Through many years, Rooney would call on local help and friends from his other endeavors to help manage various aspects of the team. Early and often he called on Walt Kiesling. Walt was willing to do most anything to help the cause.

The first decade of the team's existence proved a woeful financial and athletic exercise for Rooney. He was no talent scout and those he relied on to help were no better. Rooney didn't have a franchise player like Red Grange to help him out of his financial stew, but he did have a miraculous day at the track that would put him on solid financial ground for the foreseeable future. In the summer of 1936 at Saratoga Springs, Rooney came close to "sweeping the card"[5] and won over $250,000. Rooney could play the ponies! Rooney would later explain that he would have never bet the racehorses had he not done a lot of research and gave himself a good chance to win. He may have taken risks, but he was astute at what he did.

Anxious to see his team have a winning season, Rooney decided to roll the dice for his football team. The next several years would see a parade of colorful characters join his organization.

Blood and Whizzer

In 1937, Rooney hired Johnny "Blood" McNally to run the team. Blood was a talented running back, but was footloose and wild. He was a poet, a public speaker, merchant seaman, bartender, hotel desk clerk, cryptographer, economics professor, and Pro Hall of Fame football player.[6] He had driven Green Bay Coach Curly Lambeau to distraction before joining Pittsburgh.

Blood would coach a couple seasons and end up resigning during the third. Under his watch the Pittsburgh fans had one fascinating season due to the extraordinary play of a young wonder, Byron "Whizzer" White. White was a potential superstar, but he was headed straight to Oxford as a Rhodes Scholar when Art Rooney attempted to delay him for a time in Pittsburgh. Rooney waved

$15,800 in front of Whizzer, who paused, but still decided to cross the pond. Rooney sent Blood to persuade White to take the money. Eventually, White decided a detour to Pittsburgh would work.

White played inspired ball in the 1938 season and won the rookie of the year honors along with the league rushing title. Everything White did was exceptional because he put exceptional effort into everything he did. However, the Steelers were just 2–9 for the season. Blood would credit the team's constant change in personnel for their poor performance.

After one season, White went to Oxford, but returned to the league in 1940–41 playing for the Detroit Lions to earn enough to pay for law school. Before attending law school, he joined the Navy at the outset of World War II. He met future President John F. Kennedy, worked for his administration, and was called on to serve on the Supreme Court. Justice Byron White would remain there for 31 years.

War Years

In the 1940s, Art Rooney's Steelers along with other teams suffered financially as players went off to war and the public interest in the game declined. Of those who did play, some had injuries that precluded them from military service—poor eyesight, chronic leg injuries, etc.—but they were able to play football. Some professional players were also preoccupied with full-time jobs to back the war effort.

In a few instances teams merged for a season at a time to control costs. In 1943, the Steelers and Eagles became the Steagles. In 1944, the Steelers and the Cardinals became the Card-Pitts. It was not easy for teams to share players and for coaches from two different teams to work together. No doubt, it was also a challenge to come up with cheers for the Card-Pitts.

In 1946 as the war ended, Rooney brought in Jock Sutherland, the legendary taskmaster of the Pittsburgh (College) Panthers to coach. Sutherland was just the right man for the job—honest and tough. According to Dan Rooney, Sutherland's football was "rockem-sockem coal miner football."[7] Sutherland's great reputation helped the Steelers to sell season tickets. Sales jumped from 1,500 to 22,000 after he was named new head coach.[8] Sutherland preferred a single wing attack used in college versus the T formation that had gained acceptance in the pros. He made it work in Pittsburgh because he drilled his players to perform it perfectly.

After having won just one game in 1945, the Steelers went 5–5–1 in Sutherland's first year, 1946. In his second year, they leapfrogged to an 8–4 record. The Steelers tied for the division lead and lost to the Eagles in their first playoff. Pittsburgh fans were looking forward to the next season. Sadly, Sutherland died from a heart attack before the next season got underway.

Hopes of a championship did not immediately slip away. John Michelosen, a young protégé of Sutherland, took over, but the Steelers dropped to 4–8 in 1948. They improved to 6–5–1 in 1949. The Steelers picked up Jim Finks in the 1949 draft, giving them an excellent pass combination of Finks to tight end Ebbie Nickel that would please the fans in the early-to-mid 50s. Rooney also added tailbacks Bobby Gage and Joe Geri, who would help entertain the fans. Unfortunately, the Steelers would get no closer to the championship under Michelosen's tenure, which lasted through 1951. He held tight to Sutherland's single-wing offense and could not make it work in the pros.

1950s and 1960s

Art Rooney's sons were coming of age during the 50s. He was strict with his sons, but he and his wife provided a good home for them. Dan Rooney, the eldest son, recalled that his dad wanted his kids to be solid characters and spiritually grounded. Art wanted his kids to grow up strong. His boys were athletic and he didn't allow crying and complaining. He was busy with all his business ventures, but at times he played football and baseball with the boys. He also taught them some boxing rudiments. But Art was a tough critic when he watched them play.[9]

He preached the importance of integrity and character. He would not permit them to criticize others. "That isn't going to do you or that person any good talking like that," he would say.[10] "My father used to tell us boys," said

Art Jr., "Treat everybody the way you'd like to be treated. Give them the benefit of the doubt, but never let anyone mistake kindness for weakness."[11]

In 1951, the Steelers drafted one of the most fearsome defensive players of the day, future Hall of Famer Ernie Stautner of Boston College, a man who put the steel in the Steelers. Stautner would play 14 seasons for Rooney's team and be elected a Pro Bowl player nine times.

A well-seasoned Joe Bach returned to coach the Steelers in 1952. Bach, who had been fired 15 years earlier, changed the offense from the single wing to the T formation. It didn't seem to help. The Steelers went 5–7. In 1953, the Steelers went 6–6 and Bach was out again due to illness.

One highlight of Bach's tenure was young Jim Finks's coming of age. He passed for 2,308 yards and 20 touchdowns in 1952. Finks would play for six years and then go on to become one of the most admired and successful sports executives and Hall of Famer.

In addition to Finks's 20-touchdown season performance in 1952, Lynn Chandnois's heroics in a game against the Giants was memorable. Chandnois returned the opening kickoff for 97 yards, but it was called back on a penalty. According to Chandnois, the referee Lloyd Brazil was from his home town of Flint, Michigan, and they chatted briefly as the ball was being teed-up for the second time. Brazil joked to Chandnois, "let's see you take this one back too." To the amazement of everyone,

Chandnois took the second kick all the way back for a touchdown as well. After the play, Rooney later reported that Assistant Coach Walt Kiesling, who was apparently stingy with his praise, said, "Isn't Chandnois the luckiest guy you ever saw in your life?" When Rooney told Chandnois about Kiesling's comment, Chandnois laughed and told Rooney, "I guess I was lucky both times."[12] After Bach's exit, Rooney brought old reliable, Walt Kiesling, in as head coach. It was Kiesling's third time around. In 1954, the Steelers went 4–8 and then followed with two 5–7 years–1955 and 1956. Critics saw Kiesling as stubborn and predictable. He also shied away from taking risks. But Kiesling had proven his loyalty to Rooney many times.

Art's sons promoted the drafting of a young University of Louisville quarterback named Johnny Unitas. Unitas was a Pittsburgh native, which generally held sway with Rooney, who liked homegrown talent. The Steelers drafted Unitas, but Kiesling cut him without giving him a chance to play in preseason.[13]

The Steelers acquired a winning coach in Raymond "Buddy" Parker in 1957. Parker was a good football man, but he would prove to be a headstrong skipper. He had little patience with young players and preferred proven veterans. At times he would let his emotions overrule logic and make rash decisions. During his tenure, he recruited ex-Lions quarterback Bobby Layne, who had just recovered from a broken leg.

Layne was from Texas and spoke with a pronounced drawl. He was unruly and would frequently stay out all night before a game. But he could always manage to perform well. He was a superb leader on the field, always cool and collected, but entirely committed to winning. Everyone around him believed in him.

The Steelers went 6–6 in 1957 and, with Layne, improved to 7–4–1 in 1958 and 6–5–1 in 1959. They were a promising team heading into the new decade, but didn't quite get there under Parker. Parker continued to coach the Steelers with mixed results through the 1964 season. He would often quit only to be talked into staying by Art Rooney. As the team approached the 1965 season, Parker quit again, but this time Rooney accepted his resignation—it was time to move on. Mike Nixon was promoted to head coach, but after a drab 2–12 season, Bill Austin was brought in recording a 5–8–1 mark for 1966, a 4–9–1 mark for 1967 and a 2–11–1 mark for 1968.

Going into 1969 Rooney and his sons spent a great deal of time seeking just the right coach to turn things around. By this time Art had handed over much of the responsibilities of running the team to son Dan. But Art was still involved, especially in big moves. He had also become the "Chief" to those around him—conceivably an indication that although there were other Rooney men helping to run the Steelers, there was only one Chief. No one debated Art's rulings. Rooney had always been a delegator, not a meddler, but when something bubbled up to the top for his approval, he was decisive and conclusive.[14]

Perhaps Rooney was thinking about Sutherland's success when he tried to sign a young Joe Paterno, who looked very impressive in the run he had at Penn State. Paterno came within an eyelash away of taking the professional football salary he was offered, but decided to stick it out with the Nittany Lions in State College where he knew he would have more control of the program.[15]

Noll and the 1970s

Rooney's next coach selection was Chuck Noll, who was working with Don Shula in Baltimore. Noll was a great talent and came highly recommended by Shula. Noll came from another northern industrial city: Cleveland. But rather than boxing and gambling like Rooney, his tastes included classical music and wine. Rather than a storyteller like Rooney, Noll was a "get to the point" kind of guy. He had been well-schooled in football and was ready for the job. The elder Rooney saw to it that Noll was given authority to build the team his way. Noll's Steelers started out slowly with a 1–13 season in 1969. However, 1969 began an incredible turning point for the Steelers. Noll had little input on the 1969 draft because he came in just before it, but for the next several years the Steelers drafted a number of future Hall of Famers: Joe Greene (1969); Terry Bradshaw, Mel

Blount (1970); Jack Ham (1971); Franco Harris (1972); Lynn Swann, Jack Lambert, John Stallworth, and Mike Webster (1974).

The defining moment that seemed to end the string of frustration and put the Steelers into a new winning way came in the AFC divisional playoff game on December 23, 1972. Pittsburgh had the ball on its own 20-yard line with just 1 minute 20 seconds to go. Five plays later, the Steelers were still 60 yards from pay dirt with only 22 seconds remaining. Bradshaw threw to "Frenchy" Fuqua over the middle, but Raiders defensive back Jack Tatum crashed into Fuqua and the ball with such force at the point of contact the ball flew backward like it had actually been passed by some unknown hand. Franco Harris made a superb athletic move to grab the ball off his shoelaces and alluded tacklers on his way to the end zone for the score and the win.

Although the Steelers lost the AFC Championship to the Dolphins, they made an impression with football fans, their competitors, and—most importantly—themselves. Rooney's Steelers were winners.

In 1973, the Steelers were improved, but streaky. They went 8–1 to start, but lost 3 in a row down the stretch making the playoffs, but having a rematch with the Raiders on their turf. It was too much to overcome and the Raiders got revenge for the Immaculate Reception game of 1972, winning 33–14.

Everything came together for Art Rooney's team in 1974. The Steelers defense came of age and quarterback

Terry Bradshaw hit his stride. They waltzed through the playoffs and won Rooney his first championship in 42 years of ownership. They faced a solid Minnesota Vikings team under Bud Grant, but the Steel Curtain defense made them look anemic. Steelers won Super Bowl IX 16–6.

In 1975, the Steelers made it back to the Super Bowl. Behind 10–7 after three quarters, they overtook the Cowboys in a tough defensive match 21–17.

The Steelers nemesis, the Oakland Raiders, defeated them in the 1976 AFC Championship game. Late season key injuries on offense kept them from full strength. What followed in 1977 were distractions, right from the preseason. A lawsuit filed against Coach Noll, labor disputes, and injuries led to a 9–5 season.

In 1978, the Steelers had it all. They went 14–2 for the season and crushed the Broncos 33–10 and Oilers 34–5 in the AFC playoffs. They beat a gifted Dallas Cowboys team 35–31 in Super Bowl XIII.

The 12–4 Steelers had their hands full in Super Bowl XIV, with the Rams leading 19–17 at the end of the third quarter. Bradshaw led his team to two scores in the final quarter to win 31–19. The Steelers had won four Super Bowls in six years.

The Steelers were not a dominant team in the 1980s. After early postseason exits in 1982 and 1983, they advanced to the AFC Championship game in 1984, but lost to Miami 45–28. Three disappointing seasons followed. As the team was preparing for the 1988 season in

August, Art Rooney died from a stroke. He had lived 87 hope-filled years. He was devoted to his family, his community, and his team.

The Steelers were back in the post season in 1989, but Denver eliminated them 24–23 in a tight divisional playoff loss. It would be Noll's last postseason run. In 1992, Bill Cowher replaced Chuck Noll who retired after amassing a record of 209–156–1 and four Super Bowls wins.

After early postseason exits in 1992 and 1993, Cowher's Steelers fought their way to the AFC Championship Game, but were bested by the Chargers 17–13. Another Super Bowl appearance marked the 1995 season when the Steelers beat the Bills and the Colts in the playoffs before losing to the Cowboys 27–17 in Super Bowl XXX.

In 1996, the Steelers advanced to the divisional playoff round where they lost to the New England Patriots. They advanced further in 1997, but lost to Denver in the AFC Championship. After losing seasons in 1998 and 1999, the Steelers improved to 9–7 in 2000.

In 2001, they advanced to the AFC Championship only to lose to the Patriots 24–17. In 2002, the Steelers postseason ended with a loss to the Tennessee Titans in a divisional playoff game. The Steelers 2003 season ended at 6-10, but they marched back in 2004 with an incredible 15-1 record. A 41–27 loss to the New England Patriots in the AFC Championship game ended their remarkable season. After a slow start in 2005, the Steelers fought through three hostile away games in the playoffs to meet and defeat the Seattle Seahawks, 21–10, in Super Bowl XL for their fifth title.

After an 8-8 season in 2006, Bill Cowher stepped down having amassed a 161–99–1 record. Mike Tomlin took over and his 2007 team advanced to the wild-card round where they lost to the Jaguars 10–7. The Steelers outgunned their playoff opponents in 2008 on their way to another Super Bowl win. They beat the Cardinals 27–23 to become Super Bowl XLIII champions. In 2009, the Steelers ended the season with a 9–7 mark.

The remarkable Steelers are built in the image of their founder, Art Rooney; they begin each season with hope and come out slugging in every contest.

Man of Faith

Art Rooney was a devout man. His faith was strong. It was an important part of his life at an early age. When his mother was ill during the flu pandemic, he sat in church all day long praying for her. When she recovered, he kept praying and going to Mass regularly throughout his entire life. [16]

Rooney was a saloon-keeper's son. He saw the good and the raw side of life on the streets. Although he became a wealthy man, he was humble. He wanted to help people and did. He saw race differently than others. He extended his family rather than isolated it.

When raising his children, Art whistled to his children and whoever else was playing in the backyard in the evening to come inside and say the rosary. If any kid protested that he was not a Catholic, Art cupped a hand around the back of his head and barked "Come on. It won't hurt you."[17] He expected his sons to show reverence....Art kept a bowl of rosary beads on the dining room table. The Rooney house was a popular destination for young boys despite Art's rigorous religious ways.

According to his friend, Bishop Donald Weur,[18] "He was a friend of politicians, thugs, and thieves, of people good and evil...and the three qualities that he possessed that left the most lasting impression were his humanity, his courage, and his charity."[19]

Like the Sisters who taught him at St. Peter's, Rooney thought it inappropriate to publicize ones charitable ways. Many stories came out after his death of what he had done for others quietly. Art's brother, Dan who had been ordained Father Silas, also offered Art some opportunities for charity. Father Silas was a missionary in China who was known to rescue women from rape, and babies from extermination. He ran an orphanage that needed a new roof. Art obliged.[20]

Every day was a day of worship, prayer, and thanksgiving. He was taught to practice the Corporal Works of Mercy: to feed the hungry, to clothe the naked, give drink to the thirsty, shelter the homeless, tend the sick, visit those in prison, and bury the dead. He attended wakes frequently and paid for burials of the poor and homeless. He wanted the expenses of his own funeral kept under $1,000.[21]

Rooney "kept the faith" in many ways. The ancient practice of visiting seven churches on Holy Thursday was another tradition kept by Rooney and still continued in Pittsburgh. It originated in Rome where pilgrims visited the seven major basilicas: Saint John Lateran, Saint Peter, Saint Mary Major, Saint Paul-outside-the-Walls, Saint Lawrence-outside-the-Walls, Saint Sebastian-outside-the-Walls, and Holy Cross-in-Jerusalem.

Those who knew Art and the man himself would insist that he was no saint. But he had strong religious convictions and put them to practice every day. He also passed those convictions down to the next generation. The Rooney family continues to fight the good fight and keep the faith.

Hope for Maryville: Father John P. Smyth

A former All-American basketball player at Notre Dame University, John Smyth was a first-round draft choice of the Saint Louis Hawks (now Atlanta Hawks) professional basketball team. Smyth was born in Chicago, where he attended DePaul Academy.

Smyth elected to forego a professional basketball career and entered the seminary instead. Upon his ordination in 1962, he was assigned to Maryville Academy.

Legendary sportswriter Bill Gleason once quipped, "John Smyth was a first-round draft choice in the National Basketball Association. He had to choose between the NBA and the Archdiocese of Chicago. He decided to go for the money. Little did he know they would give him an orphanage."[22]

Father Smyth was named executive director of Maryville in 1970. However, the archdiocese had determined to close the facility because it was no longer financially viable and its buildings were in disrepair. Smyth saved the facility by reaching out to other funding sources using his considerable power of persuasion. Smyth's fundraising talents and selfless dedication to Maryville's children became legendary. He developed several multimillion dollar events that helped revitalize the facility and manage the growing needs of its constituency. Sports stars, movie stars, rock stars, civic leaders, business owners, and celebrities of all kinds knew of his work and supported Maryville.

There Is a Hope that Burns Within

Smyth created innovations that gave the children more of a role in their living space and tried to emulate a family surrounding. He also emphasized sports and activities that would encourage the children to grow and develop self-esteem. Former students often commented that once they entered Maryville, they felt safe for the first time in their lives. Family involvement was encouraged, but if not possible, the staff, including Father Smyth, did their best to encourage the students in a personal way.

The state now emphasizes keeping children with their families (even troubled families) as much as possible and sending other socially and emotionally capable children to foster homes. This has meant that the youth attending Maryville and other like-kind facilities are typically more seriously troubled. A quarter century into Father Smyth's directorship, Maryville had taken on increasingly complicated cases and when a teenage suicide and assaults took place within a short time span, the State of Illinois withdrew its wards. Other institutions of its type have experienced similar problems.

Father Smyth stepped down from the directorship in 2004, but he still resides at Maryville and continues his pastoral duties with the community of Maryville-Our Lady of Guadalupe Shrine. Smyth also continues to head the Maryville Foundation. The Foundation uses donations to pay for postsecondary school for any Maryville alumnus who is admitted to a college or vocational training program.[23]

Under Sister Catherine Ryan, former head of the juvenile division of the Cook County States Attorney's Office, Maryville relies more on treatment and clinical care for its troubled children.[24]

During his long service, Maryville expanded from its original charter of caring and educating dependent

JOHN SMYTH TURNED DOWN PROFESSIONAL
BASKETBALL FOR HIS KIDS

youth. Services today include: residential programs, behavioral and mental health services, family support services, secondary and special education, and community development programs. New additions in the past few years include Maryville Crisis Nursery and the Children's Healthcare Center.

In July 2005 Father Smyth established the Standing Tall Charitable Foundation to provide educational and vocational training scholarships and to issue monetary awards to institutions whose purposes coincide with and further the foundation's mission, with emphasis on assisting those most at risk and in need. The name and logo were inspired by a sentiment expressed by Father Smyth for many years: "No person stands so tall as the one who stoops to help a child."[25]

In March of 2007, Father Smyth was appointed president of Notre Dame College Prep in Niles, Illinois. In 2009, Sports Faith International inducted Smyth into the Sports Faith Hall of Fame. SFI also created the Fr. John P. Smyth Award in honor of the man whose life bears testimony to the world-changing power of combining the virtues and influence of sports with mountain-moving faith.[26] This honor is awarded annually to an outstanding Catholic athlete or coach interested in pursuing a religious vocation.

MARYVILLE AND ME

Art Contreras arrived at Maryville Academy on February 14, 1955, at 2:30 p.m. He was six years old and his parents were divorced because of alcoholism. Maryville is two miles from my childhood home in Des Plaines. My parents encouraged their children to give one of their Christmas presents to a Maryville resident. We took that as a mandate. One Christmas I got a new baseball glove and gave it to Maryville. Next spring, Art was wearing the mitt when he struck me out.

My heroes are those who accept God's grace and mercy and forgive those who trespass against them. "Art, I am not bitter."

When I complained about the conditions in my home once, my mother replied, "How would you like to live at Maryville for a while?" The idea was somewhat intriguing because Maryville had excellent athletic teams!

I was on the Des Plaines Park District football teams and the St. Mary's Grammar School basketball and baseball teams. We played in a basketball league in the Maryville gymnasium on Saturday afternoons. We never beat Maryville's A teams.

Art played quarterback and safety in football; guard in basketball; and pitcher in baseball. As a sixth grader, he started on the eighth grade basketball team. When I was in sixth grade, the St. Mary's eighth grade team did not win a game. When I was in seventh grade,

I started at forward on the eighth grade team. We had one victory. St. Joseph the Worker got way ahead and put in its second string. Before the team could recover, we won 14–12. We lost to St. James 46–1. I led the team in scoring.

Father Smyth coached Maryville's 1962 eighth grade football team to a 26–1 record. The team often played two games in one day. I was the quarterback of the 1962 Rand Park heavyweight football team that went 0–9. Later on in eighth grade, I started at center for the St. Mary's basketball team. We were 15–7: 8–3 at Maryville.

During the regular season, Maryville beat us 44–25 and 44–30. At the end of the season, we beat the Maryville B team 46–43 in the Don Bosco Tournament. Art and the Maryville A team were busy in another tournament.

Several years ago Art told me, "You never really leave Maryville. Father Smyth is always there for counseling. Maryville as a home has been very good to any kid who has gone out there. I just want Maryville to be there for some other kid who might come along and need help at the same stage in young adulthood." That's why Art regularly worked Maryville's Chuckwagon Day. With a staff of 300 people, he would feed everyone. He was involved since the event's inception in 1973. A thousand people were expected in the gym. 2,500 attended. Later Chuckwagon Days attracted more than 10,000 diners who ate over 25,000 sandwiches: hamburgers, hot dogs, brats, Italian sausage; 15,000 pieces of chicken; 3,500 pounds of ribs; 1,500 pounds of beef; 1,500 pounds of salads; 5,000 orders of nachos; 10,000 ice cream bars; 50,000 pieces of candy—all consumed in five hours. The scriptural precedent was the multiplication of the loaves and the fishes. It's difficult for me, but I publicly acknowledge that Art was a better basketball player than I. Of course, he had his own gym.

FATHER BRADLEY

Father William Bradley was born December 7, 1941, in County Donegal, Ireland. When he was in high school, he ran the half mile under two minutes and the mile in 4:23.0. During his college and seminary years, he was not allowed to compete outside his school.

Since 1974, Father Bradley has taught religion, math, and physical education and coached track at Saint Michael's High School in Dublin. In 1984, he ran a marathon and then continued running 20 miles a week. Because he was on summer leave at Saint John the Baptist Church in Fort Lauderdale, Florida, he was available to say Mass for the Chicago Bears before their preseason game with the Miami Dolphins on August 14, 1989.

In his homily, Father Bradley said:

> The people here before me certainly know they have to use the talents that they have. Just like becoming a good person, it doesn't come by

accident. You needed discipline and dedication and goals and a lot of patience with yourselves and other people. We can't be perfect. Sometimes we get disgusted because we don't achieve success as quickly as we would like.

A person is successful if he is on the first team of a good football team. Some don't give as much as they have. Success is overcoming the obstacles that are before you. That's what God is calling you to be: the best you possibly can be. It's a great privilege to be in that position. People want to talk with you and get your autograph. People look up to you, especially young people. They are going to imitate you. That's an awesome responsibility.

Saint Paul had a similar burden. God said to him, "My grace is sufficient for you." He says the same to you.

You are not perfect. The important thing about failure is to start again. Sport is one of the greatest things to unite people. In my country, there is a divide in Ireland. Rugby surmounts the divide. They look upon themselves as followers of sport. You can unite people. You can help people be better than themselves. Your vocation is a calling. Accept the talents that you have been given. Use them and believe in God as well.

— ENDNOTES —

1 United States Conference of Catholic Bishops, *United States Catholic Catechism for Adults* (Washington, DC: USCC Publishing Services, 2006), 499.
2 Dan Rooney, Andrew E. Masich, and David F. Halaas, *Dan Rooney, My 75 Years with the Pittsburgh Steelers and the NFL* (New York: Da Capo Press, 2007), 10.
3 Rooney, Masich, and Halaas, *Dan Rooney, My 75 Years with the Pittsburgh Steelers and the NFL,* 11.
4 Arthur J. Rooney, Jr. with Roy McHugh, *Ruanaidh: The Story of Art Rooney and His Clan,* 2nd Ed. (Pittsburgh: Art Rooney Jr. Publishing, 2008), 15.
5 "Sweeping the card" is picking the winner in each race.
6 Dennis J. Gullickson, *Vagabond Halfback: The Life and Times of Johnny "Blood" McNally* (Neenah, WI: Trails Books (Big Earth Publishing), 2006), xii.
7 Rooney, Masich, and Halaas, *Dan Rooney, My 75 Years with the Pittsburgh Steelers and the NFL,* 39.
8 Rooney, Masich, and Halaas, *Dan Rooney: My 75 Years with the Pittsburgh Steelers and the NFL,* 35.
9 Rooney, Masich, and Halaas, *Dan Rooney: My 75 Years with the Pittsburgh Steelers and the NFL,* 19–20.
10 Rooney, Masich, and Halaas, *Dan Rooney: My 75 Years with the Pittsburgh Steelers and the NFL,* 26.
11 Freeman, Lew, *Pittsburgh Steelers, The Complete History* (Minneapolis: MBI Publishing Company, 2009), 12
12 Wexell, Jim, *Pittsburgh Steelers, Men of Steel* (Champaign, IL: Sports Publishing LLC, 2006), 13.
13 Rooney with McHugh, *Ruanaidh: The Story of Art Rooney and His Clan,* 142.
14 Rooney with McHugh, *Ruanaidh: The Story of Art Rooney and His Clan,* 242.
15 Joe Paterno with Bernard Asbell, *Paterno: By the Book* (New York: Berkley, 1991) 6.
16 Rob Ruck, Maggie Jones Patterson, and Michael P. Weber, *Rooney: A Sporting Life* (Lincoln, NE: University of Nebraska, 2010), 84.
17 Ruck, Patterson, and Weber, *Rooney: A Sporting Life,* 255.
18 Weur has been named a cardinal by Pope Benedict XVI.
19 Ruck, Patterson, and Weber, *Rooney: A Sporting Life,* 520.
20 Rooney with McHugh, *Ruanaidh: the Story of Art Rooney and His Clan,* 38–39.

[21] Ruck, Patterson, and Weber, *Rooney: A Sporting Life*, 520.

[22] Bill Gleason's banquet speech included this story.

[23] Michelle Martin, "Maryville Academy Celebrates 125 Years," *Catholic New World,* August 17, 2008.

[24] Ames Boykin, "Maryville at 125: A Look Back and Ahead," *Daily Herald,* July 27, 2008.

[25] Quote is the official slogan of the Standing Tall Foundation and is attributed to Father John Smyth. Standing Tall Foundation, viewed at http://www.standingtallfoundation.org/aboutus.html (accessed October 27, 2010).

[26] Sports Faith International, Press Release: "Sports Faith International Teams Up with Catholic Athletes for Christ, Relevant Radio, and Catholic Knights to Announce Inductees to the 2009 Sports Faith Hall of Fame," February 2, 2009, viewed at http://www.sportsfaithinternational.com/ (accessed on October 27, 2010).

RUNNING ON THE MASTERS' CIRCUIT

OH HAPPY DAY

NANCY SWIDER PELTZ AT
1984 SARAJEVO OLYMPIC GAMES

There is certain irony in sports and life that can make us laugh and cry. It is a sense of incongruity that exists between what we want for ourselves and what actually unfolds. Why do we so often end up in a destination that was not part of our travel plans? Many learn to accept that someone else is steering the boat that we are rowing.

MY OLYMPIAN FRIEND

On May 2, 1978, I accepted Nancy Swider into my life. She said the closing prayer at the Chicago Fellowship of Christian Athletes' Spring Banquet. She praised God with her prayer and with her appearance. She also honored her father and her mother.

So I called her home on Home Avenue in Park Ridge, Illinois frequently. Her mother usually answered. Quick on the uptake, I often said, "Hello, Mrs. Swider, this is Pat McCaskey."

She would reply, "Oh, hi, Tom."

Nancy and I attended Bear Bible studies together that fall. Then she went to Inzell, West Germany, for speedskating training. After she had returned home, she chastised me for making my transatlantic phone calls to her. Later that day, I received the bill.

The following year, on April 5, 1979, we went to a Bears Bible study on a night when the wind was so strong that windows were blown out of the Hancock Building in downtown Chicago. During the drive back to Nancy's home, my car died. Fortunately, some hippies in a pick-up truck gave us a ride back to Doug and Nancy Planks' home. One of the songs on the truck radio was, "Gonna Take a Lot of Love."

The Planks loaned us one of their cars and then met the tow truck at my car. After the car had been repaired, I marked the words "winter hopes" above the left front tire.

This was a tribute to Nancy's diligent training. She was the most dedicated athlete I had ever met.

My Bible studies continued. At the end of November, I sent her a telegram. "Just finished reading the Bible. The Christians won."

Olympic Times

The first time ever I saw her skate was Thursday December 6, 1979. I visited with Milwaukee reporters prior to the Bears' game at Green Bay the following Sunday. (The Bears won 15–14.) Then I watched Nancy work out on the Olympic-sized skating rink in West Allis, which is right next to Milwaukee. She often commuted 250 miles a day in order to skate there.

Nancy's commitment to skating reflects the approach that her entire family takes to athletics and life. I had raved so much to my family about the Swiders that by Christmas of 1979 my family wrapped me in swaddling clothes and put me on their doorstep.

Nancy had competed in the 1976 Olympics in Innsbruck. At the end of December, I saw her skate in the Olympic trials. She made her second Olympics. Nancy was an alternate for the 1980 Winter Olympics. On March 16, 1980, she set a world record with 17:27.55 for 10,000 meters. A little over two months later on Saturday, May 17, we competed in the Gil Dodds 10,000-meter run at Wheaton College. The next day, we competed in the Park Ridge 10,000-meter run.

Nancy is a complete athlete. On December 6, 1980, I saw her compete for the Wheaton College swimming team at the University of Chicago. The next day, the Bears beat the Green Bay Packers 61–7 at Soldier Field.

1981 was a rebuilding year for our friendship. Cupid's arrow is often different from God's plan.

The first time ever I heard her speak was April 4, 1981. Nancy and I spoke at the Judson College FCA miniconference in Elgin, Illinois. On June 7, I attended her family's graduation party for her. It had taken her a while. Her father's banner across the front of the Swider home proclaimed, "Congratulations Princess, Wheaton College 1974–81."

On March 12, 1982, Nancy visited Halas Hall at Lake Forest College. She received some advice about her injured knee. Then, after much deliberation and prayer, she had arthroscopic surgery.

Before Nancy spoke at the Chicago FCA Spring Banquet on May 6, we made a deal. When she asked rhetorical questions during her speech, I promised not to raise my hand as if I knew the answer. In return, I did not want to hear any "uhms" and "you knows" from her.

During Swider family volleyball games that summer, she would often yell, "I got it." I was forced to correct her with, "I have it."

Nancy was dating Wheaton College assistant football coach, Jeff Peltz, in early January 1983 when I saw her take second place overall in the national speedskating championships in West Allis. It was quite a successful comeback after her surgery. I said to Nancy and some of Jeff's friends, "Nancy has matured a lot since she has been dating Jeff."

Ted Carlson, one of Jeff's friends replied, "They're both pretty strong-headed." Jeff captained the 1980 Wheaton College football team and he still holds the school record for sacks.

On Super Bowl Sunday, 1983, on the suggestion of Mrs. Swider, the Bradleys and Swiders arranged for me to meet Gretchen Wagle, who later became my wife.

On Saturday, April 23, Nancy and I spoke at Judson College again. I was busy keeping track of her "uhms" and "you knows." She praised God with her remarks and with her appearance.

A week later, Nancy had a custom-made birthday cake that was covered with Bible quotes planted in my office at Halas Hall. I was tempted to have it shellacked and take it on tour, but I did not yield. I was also tempted to take it to the FCA Spring Banquet on Thursday, May 6. Instead, I had this poem published in the banquet program.

In His Steps

For to this you have been called, because Christ also suffered for you, leaving you an example that you should follow in his footsteps.

—1 Peter 2:21

We are not called
To walk on water
Or change water into wine
Or multiply loaves and fishes
Or raise the dead
Or be scourged
At the pillar
Or walk
To Calvary
With a cross
On which
To be crucified.
We are not called
To do
What is impossible
For us.
Christ performed all
Of those heavenly deeds
At a three-year pace.
It is
For us
To follow
In His steps.
Live for righteousness
Without being self-righteous.

—Patrick McCaskey

Olympic Family

In December and January, I made five trips to West Allis to watch Nancy skate. She made her third Olympics and finished second overall. Instead of going to the Olympics myself, I decided to use my two weeks of vacation for my honeymoon.

After a 10th place in the Olympic 3,000 meters, Nancy finished first overall in the four-event Golden Skates Championships in Inzell. She won the 1500, the 3000, and the 5000.

Then her father had the best comment about Nancy's future. He said, "She has a lot of irons in the fire, but she doesn't like to iron."

On Saturday, May 11, 1985, Jeff Peltz and Nancy married at South Park Church in Park Ridge, Illinois. At the reception, I told them, "Marriage is easy; God does most of the work."

In lieu of flowers, donations were made to the Chicago Fellowship of Christian Athletes.

On July 4, we ran the first annual Swider Mile at Maine South High School in Park Ridge. Nancy's brother Mike was first; Nancy's husband Jeff was second; and I was third. Nancy finished first among the women.

On July 4, 1986, Mike was first and I was second. Jeff did not run because of a leg broken while waterskiing. Nancy did not run because of what she called a pulled hamstring. It turned out that she was pregnant with her

NANCY SWIDER PELTZ JR. AT OLYMPIC GAMES

daughter Nancy Junior, who like her mother, would grow up to compete as an Olympic speedskater.

On July 4, 1987, Mike was first and I was second in the Swider mile. Nancy was first again among the women. This inspired her to train for speedskating again. My wife, her parents, and my son Ed and I had the privilege of seeing Nancy make her fourth Olympic speedskating team. No other speedskater had ever done that for the United States.

After the competition, we were sitting in the warming house before we went to dinner. Nancy asked, "What are we waiting for?"

I replied, "The Second Coming."

I value my friendship with the Swiders. They are a dedicated and devout family.

When Jesus Washed Our Sins Away

It seems ironic that for Christians our "Happy Day" is the day Christ was crucified. Yet it is the day "when Jesus washed our sins away." As Saint Paul wrote, "I have been crucified with Christ, and I live now not with my own life but with the life of Christ who lives in me. The life I now live in this body I live in faith: faith in the Son of God who loved me and who sacrificed himself for my sake."

It is Christ's death that redeems us. And we know that in death there is life; death is not the end of the story.

Coach Swider's Life and Faith

Nancy's father, John, was a coach and teacher in the Chicago public school system for 37 years and spent 23 years at Taft High School as freshman-sophomore football and swimming coach. In 1981 and 1982, under Coach Swider, Taft won the Public League speedskating title.[1] Coach Swider was a tremendous example and guide to his student athletes in sport and a man of remarkable faith.

John Swider passed away on June 9, 1991. His funeral was held on Tuesday, June 11 at 11:00 a.m. at South Park Church. The funeral program included this:

> He was a man who at the age of 43, made his most important decision when he put Jesus Christ first in his life. His unparalleled love and commitment to his wife and children has been the foundation of his family's cohesiveness. He loved and served his country with a passion. He was and will remain forever his family's stalwart leader.

Pastor Gay announced that all of John's children would talk about their father to the congregation.

Nancy said:

> Last year I wanted to write an article about my father and have him find it in the local newspaper. Two Thursdays ago it was in the paper. My father found it the last Thursday of his life.

It read, "Every day is Father's Day." To be a father is to love unconditionally. He had a tough love. When I was born, my father wanted me to be a third son. Instead of calling me Buddy, he called me Princess.

He would bring a teacher roses on Washington's birthday. He taught me respect for authority. My father has also sacrificed for me to achieve my goals. No request was too much for him. He never failed to respond to my senses. Nothing would stand in my father's way when he knew something was right. He was my hero.

John Junior said:

A great man must first love his Lord and his family. His family must think he is a great man. Dad was an example to all who knew him.

Every fourth of July, he raised the flag and made a vigorous speech. He was a man of few words. He never said anything he couldn't back up. Dad was a champion of subordinates. He made the secretaries at Taft High School feel like they ran the school. He put signs up before our competitions. Dad was a champion. He was a great man. I loved my Dad.

Mike said:

At times like this he would say, "How tough is tough? Let's see what you've got." On Sunday, we went to the rock at Lake Michigan where my Dad had painted the family names and the phrase, "love is forever."

In his confession of faith in 1982, he had written, "I met my wife while attending college. She introduced me to the concept of a personal relationship with God."

They [my parents] were successful in their pursuit of worldly goals, but they were more concerned that they were doing what God had in mind for them. My father never said anything to please anybody. He said what was on his mind. He hated hypocrites.

On Dad and Mom's last anniversary together, he wrote the names of the family on a card for her, "These are our best memories. I was always happy to come home. You gave me three great children. Stay tough, Del. I'll always love you. I'll always be with you."

When you're in school, you always say my Dad is the toughest. Well my Dad was the toughest. He was given a year to live. He lived 2½ more years.

He hadn't been able to get out of bed for four days. Fifteen minutes before he died, he sat in a chair and tried to eat. He died in my mother's arms. To his dying day, he got up off his back. He lived what he preached. He walked what he talked.

My wife and I are going to have a baby in August. The baby will never see my father. But I'll raise the baby to be just like my Dad.

Pastor Gay introduced Dave Wager, who spoke as a representative of the thousands of student-athletes John had coached.

Dave said:

Coach Swider was one of my heroes. Another was my father, who passed away a few years ago. Coach Swider was there to encourage me that day.

I was a cripple. I got kicked around a lot when I was in grade school. My brother was a great swimmer. I figured it was in the genes. My first race was 100 meters, four laps. The other swimmers were finished before I had done two laps. My brother and Coach Swider were there to encourage me. As a sophomore, I was undefeated.

I never knew how to play football, but Coach Swider taught me. I didn't even know how to put the equipment on. I played college football. He taught me driver's ed. Coach Swider waited for me to succeed. Others wait for people to fail.

Coach Swider said, "Dave, I believe in you." He left a great legacy. Coach Swider stepped into the lives of thousands of people and believed in them.

— Endnotes —

1   Robert Pruter, "The Glorious History of High School Speedskating in Illinois 1921 to 1988," Illinois High School Association, viewed at http://www.ihsa.org/initiatives/hstoric/speedskating.htm (accessed October 27, 2010).

EDWARD, PATRICK, THOMAS, GRETCHEN, AND JAMES McCASKEY

TWO OR MORE

GRETCHEN AND PATRICK MCCASKEY

I n team sports, the players need to act in harmony. Each individual has a role that is part of the team character. Strength and energy build as the athletes work together in a common cause—coming together as one. With group chemistry and camaraderie, the team is much greater than the sum of its parts.

This same dynamic is powerful outside the realm of sports in every other aspect of life. However, it reaches a spiritual summit when people gather in a marriage and in a faith community.

"When two or more are gathered in his name, there is love."[1]

DOCTOR WAYNE "COACH" GORDON

My wife, Gretchen Wagle McCaskey, and I have a mixed marriage. I did not attend Wheaton College, which is a very fine school as well as a bastion of Christian conservatism here in the midwest. I am willing to accept an honorary degree. I like to drive in the Wheaton College lane—the far right.

At a Wheaton College homecoming game several years ago, someone described one of its most admired alums, Wayne Gordon. The man said:

> You could be all the way down on your luck. You could have lost your job or someone in your family could have died. Gordy would listen to you, slap you on the back, remind you that God loves you, and say, "You're a good man." You'd go away feeling 100% better.

Coach was born August 25, 1953, in Fort Dodge, Iowa. He lettered in football, basketball, and track at Fort Dodge High School. He once ran 100 yards in 10 seconds flat. Coach was a four-year letterman in football at Wheaton College. He was the captain as a senior.

Coach Gordon was inspired by John Perkins's life and work—specifically how John had returned to Mississippi to minister and work with the poor in the early days of the civil rights movement. Although Perkins and Gordon came from totally different backgrounds, both are principal players in the Christian community development movement—expressing the love of Christ in America's poor communities, not at arm's length, but at the grassroots level.[2]

As Perkins himself has described it, Wayne's calling was a "burden to be the kind of Christian he thought God wanted him to be."[3] After Coach graduated from Wheaton in 1975, he moved to the Lawndale Community of Chicago—one of the most impoverished urban areas in the country. He coached football and wrestling and taught history at nearby Farragut High School. Farragut head football coach, Guido Marchetti, had long been an advocate for helping athletes grow spiritually.

Coach met former baton twirler Anne Starkey at a funeral for a mutual friend. He felt that she came to him as a gift from God. She was determined to never marry a minister or a coach. While they were going together, Coach was very eager to introduce Anne to everyone. After a few minutes of conversation, he would ask, "So, what do you think of Anne?"

Coach and Anne were married June 18, 1977. They have three children: Angela, Andrew, and Austin. It was very interesting to hear Coach and Anne in separate conversations after Andrew's birth. Coach said, "Anne had a very difficult delivery. I was very concerned about her." Anne said, "Children are such a blessing." Their children liked to be the last one to pray, but Coach and Anne taught them to take turns.

Gordon was one of the few white persons in the area when he began his Bible study group with his athletes. He lived, married, and raised a family with the people he wanted to know and to whom he was ministering. Wayne Gordon's competitive nature would not allow for failure.[4]

At the request of the people in the neighborhood, Gordon started the Lawndale Community Church. LCC bought a former Cadillac agency and converted it to a church, a health center, and a gym. To make the gym ceiling high enough, the people dug out four feet of dirt with hand shovels and hauled it out via wheelbarrows. A banner in the gym reads, "The Lawndale Miracle."

Wayne was the founding president of the Lawndale Christian Development Corporation, the arm of Lawndale Community Church that facilitates economic development, education, and housing. He is also one of the founders of the Lawndale Christian Health Center, a healthcare ministry that sees over 120,000 patients per year. Coach gets high marks for many of his ministries, but John Perkins gives him great credit for creating indigenous leaders in the community.[5]

Wayne L. Gordon is currently chairman/president of the Christian Community Development Association

(CCDA). Much of his story evokes successful community development and other ministries. However, the Coach is also a man who identifies and ministers to people one soul at a time. The Coach's ministry has been a team effort—community development involves the entire community. His family has also played a key role and has made many sacrifices for his ministry work.

In Training with Coach Gordon

When I was a bachelor, Coach and Anne adopted me. I attended their dating seminar at a Fellowship of Christian Athletes Conference in Michigan. I learned to date based on biblical principles. I was in training.

From Genesis 2:18-25, we know:

> The Lord God said: "It is not good for the man to be alone. I will make a suitable partner for him." So the Lord God formed out of the ground various wild animals and various birds of the air, and he brought them to the man to see what he would call them; whatever the man called each of them would be its name. The man gave names to all the cattle, all the birds of the air, and all the wild animals; but none proved to be the suitable partner for the man.

> So the Lord God cast a deep sleep on the man, and while he was asleep, he took out one of his

ribs and closed its place with flesh. The Lord God then built up into a woman the rib he had taken from the man. When he brought her to the man, the man said:

"'This one, at last, is bone of my bones

And flesh of my flesh;

This one shall be called 'woman.'

For out of 'her man' this one has been taken."

That is why a man leaves his father and mother and clings to his wife, and the two of them become one body.

The man and his wife were both naked, yet they felt no shame.

Coach said to me, "You need to sleep now while God is making a suitable partner for you. You are not to be on the prowl."

I spent several nights with the Gordons in their home on Ogden Avenue, enjoying their great hospitality. One hot summer night, Coach's parents were there. Only one bedroom had air conditioning. The five of us slept in that bedroom. Coach's parents had the bed. Coach, Anne, and I slept on the floor. In the morning, all of us awoke refreshed.

There Is Love

For my thirty-third birthday, my uncle, Jim McCaskey, gave me permission to date. After nine months of prayer, I met Gretchen Wagle on Super Bowl Sunday 1983. I called her the next night and said, "I have a challenge for you. My parents are celebrating their fortieth wedding anniversary next Saturday night. I'd like you to attend."

She said, "Gosh, that really is a challenge. I accept."

A few months later, in May as I approached my nine-year anniversary with the Bears, I received a raise. When I thanked my father, I said, "Now I can afford to get married."

He asked, "Are you thinking about that?"

I replied, "Yes, I am."

He said, "Well, Mrs. Siffermann is putting her house up for sale. Maybe you ought to take a look at it." (The Siffermanns and the McCaskeys grew up together on the same block in Des Plaines.)

When I thanked my mother for the raise, I said, "Now I can afford to get married."

She demanded, "You mean you weren't making enough money before to get married?"

I said, "Of course I was, Mom. That was just a little joke."

On Saturday of Memorial Day weekend, Gretchen and I took a close look at the Siffermann house. It served its purpose. After the tour, Gretchen asked me, "Why are you looking for a house?"

I crossed my mouth with the back of my right hand and muttered, "In case you want to get married."

On Memorial Day, my mother asked me, "Why are you looking for a house?" (My mother and my wife are a lot alike.)

I replied, "Because Gretchen and I are talking about getting married."

When my mother stopped crying with joy, she asked me, "How old is she, anyway?"

I replied, "She's thirty; she only looks eighteen."

My mother gave us her mother's wedding ring. This was a great surprise, a marvelous delight, and an outward sign that she approved of the idea.

Coach Gordon's Marriage Ministry

When my wife and I needed premarital counseling, Coach and Anne provided it. When we married, Coach was a concelebrant with my boyhood friend, Father Don Nevins. We got married at College Church in Wheaton. As I stood before Coach Gordon and Father Nevins, I thought, "This is how it's going to be on the Day of Judgment. I'd better be a loving husband."

Pastor Gordon and Father Nevins are a great team. Father Nevins and the Coach officiated when our children—Ed, Tom, and James—were dedicated and baptized. Coach was the dedicator and Father Nevins, the baptizer.

Coach's parents had a great marriage. Coach and Anne have a great marriage. My wife and I try to follow their examples. Let us go therefore and do likewise.

SUPER BOWLS AND WEDDINGS

At family and club meetings prior to Super Bowl XX, Mike McCaskey, the president of the Bears, said, "Try to look at the Super Bowl as you would a wedding. There is a lot of hard work in preparing for it. There are some things that go wrong. But it is a great celebration and a lot of fun and joy for everyone."

This analogy appealed to me because I am happily married. Every Super Bowl, Gretchen and I get together with the close friends who arranged for us to meet: the world-class Swiders and Bradleys. In 1986, we got together in New Orleans. The night before Super Bowl XX, my wife and I had dinner with her family and Wayne and Anne Gordon in the team hotel. I also wanted to have Father Nevins come to the Super Bowl with us.

Prior to the January 5 playoff game at Soldier Field, one of his colleagues asked Father Nevins, "Have you heard from McCaskey?"

Father Nevins replied, "No."

Before the January 12 National Football Conference (NFC) Championship Game in Chicago, his compatriot asked Father Nevins, "Have you heard from McCaskey?"

Father Nevins replied, "No, but I'm tempted to call him."

On January 13, Father Nevins said to his spiritual brother, "I heard from McCaskey."

The astonishing reply was, "No!"

Father Nevins was with us at the Super Bowl. He flew to New Orleans the day of the game and returned to Chicago immediately after the contest.

When the Chicago Bears visit all other National Football League (NFL) cities, we take the Margaret Mead approach. We can learn from primitive cultures. For our game preparation, we camped on the Mississippi River near the Mark Twain Courtyard. Many of us visited Bourbon Street, where there was a great need for missionary work.

Coach Ditka wanted me to take care of the people who really matter: the coaches and the players. My responsibility was to arrange meals, meetings, and practices. When I came into the locker room before one practice, Walter Payton told one of the security guards to check me out pretending that he didn't know me. The guard did and everyone involved had a good laugh.

When I met Jim McMahon's father, the day before the Super Bowl, I said to him, "You should have given Jim more spankings."

He replied, "I know."

One Body One Team

Before every home game, Father Nick Marro of Melrose Park, Illinois, said Mass for the team. He was also in New Orleans to say Mass for us. John Cassis was our

PAYTON—SIMPLY THE BEST

chapel speaker before every home game. He was also our chapel speaker in New Orleans. We had Mass and chapel service on both Saturday and Sunday. I had the privilege of being the lector at both Masses. At the Sunday Mass, the epistle was 1 Corinthians 12:12-30.

In his homily, Father Marro used this passage for his Super Bowl sermon. The verses describe how everyone is important to the body of Christ, the team. "The body is one and has many members, but all the members, many though they are, are one body; and so it is with Christ."

Players could easily reflect on this spiritual notion at the time because they were living the more earthly idea of working together. Throughout the season, and particularly in the week before the Super Bowl, everyone in the Bears' organization—management, coaches, and players—contributed to the championship.

It was the first Super Bowl that I had ever attended. I only want to attend Super Bowls when the Bears are there. The team held a reception after the game. Gretchen and I left the bash early—at midnight! We went back to a room we shared with Wayne and Anne Gordon. The four of us engaged in a good pillow fight—my wife was my bunker—then we talked and laughed until two o'clock in the morning. Twenty-five years later, we are still good friends and enjoy fellowship when we can. My good friends Coach and Anne Gordon are to be congratulated for thirty-five years of devout ministry. It has been my good fortune that they have found time to minister to me and my family as well.

The nine Bears players who made the Pro Bowl "had to" leave New Orleans for Hawaii early the next morning. They were not able to attend the downtown Chicago tickertape parade. For this parade, the spotlight would shine on the players who had received less attention that season. A fitting comment that, like the Super Bowl Epistle, comes from 1 Corinthians, "We honor the members we consider less honorable by clothing them with greater care, thus bestowing on the less presentable a propriety which the more presentable already have."

As Chicago literally showered its appreciation on the Bears, it reminded me of how the confetti had rained down after the wedding of Grace Kelly.

My Team

Exactly nine months after the Bears' victory in Super Bowl XX, my wife, Gretchen, and I were blessed with a son. He reported two days early. That showed good initiative. His name is Edward the cute. We think he is gifted. My father was Edward the great. We know he was gifted.

If I die before my wife does, I hope that she gets married again. But I don't want my successor to wear my Super Bowl ring. That goes to my son Thomas. Edward received my father's Super Bowl ring when he graduated from Wheaton College. All of you are witnesses. If my wife dies before I do, I might become a priest.

After the Bears had qualified for Super Bowl XLI, I was tempted to call my former girlfriends and say, "If you

had married me, you could have gone to the Super Bowl."
Then I remembered that we need to follow Christ's example in all things. After Jesus rose from the dead, He didn't
taunt the people who had rejected Him.

GATHERING THE MCCASKEYS IN HIS NAME

According to my father, Ed McCaskey, his great-grand-
father (J. P. McCaskey) looked like Santa Claus with his
great shock of white hair, his beautiful snowy beard, and
his way of laughing so that he shook from his shoulders
to his toes. J. P. was a principal of the high school in Lancaster, Pennsylvania and he started the tradition of reading the *Christmas Carol* in the McCaskey household each
Christmas. Fittingly, he also wrote a little tune called "Jolly
Old St. Nicholas." He was the mayor of Lancaster for two
terms. Eventually, they named the high school after him.

My father told us that his grandfather, E. W. McCaskey, loved Christmas, too. He graduated from West Point
in the class of 1886 with General John Joseph Pershing who
would lead the American forces in World War I. Retired
from the army, E. W. used to thrill his grandchildren with
stories of Christmas in faraway Army posts. The grandchildren's favorite was the story of E. W. serving on an Indian
reservation in the west and how his wife had borne her
first child in a tent on the reservation. One day the tent
caught fire and they faced the winter with a great hole in
the roof. The compensation came, however, on Christmas

Eve, when they were able to bundle up on the floor with their first-born and drink in the beauty of the Christmas star shining through the hole in the roof of the tent.

My father remembered his father, Dick McCaskey, as a happy man. At Christmas, he sang carols in the most beautiful voice. He let the adjoining lot of the Mc-Caskey homestead to a farmer to sell Christmas trees during a rough year to provide for a family tree and small sum of money that bought toys for under that tree. An added bonus was the price of a ton of coal that kept the house warm.

Kit from Ireland

My grandmother Kit, Irish through and through, was re-membered most lovingly. In the house there were three men, many children and my grandmother. My father remembered:

> She made Christmas beautiful with peppermint and black walnut kisses, and filled stockings in good years and bad. Most of all, she taught us to love each other.

> When I was just a tot, I used to dry the dishes and the silverware for her, and store the silver in a drawer in the kitchen cabinet. Once when I was drying the dishes I said to her, "Mother, I am always going to be married to you."

Her reply was, "Edward, some day you will meet a nice girl and fall in love and get married."

My grandmother had a deep faith and trust in God. Her favorite answer to any problem her children might have was, "That is a sign."

My father recalled:

One Sunday [my brother] Tom and I came home from caddying at the Lancaster Country Club and my dad told me mother was in the hospital. I ran to St. Joseph's and went to see her. She had miscarried twins. When I entered her room she said, "I'm all right, Edward. The Little Flower sent me a shower of roses."[6]

After high school I enrolled in Franklin and Marshall College. Howard Herr's gas station was close to the campus. While going to class I worked 48 hours a week in the gas station for the princely sum of 15 cents an hour. Thanksgiving Day was very special that year. I was sitting in the gas station with no radio and no customers, and feeling very blue because I was missing Thanksgiving dinner. Kit [My mother] solved that. When the bus stopped in front of our house, she gave the driver a great platter of food and when he stopped at the gas station, he gave me my Thanksgiving Day dinner!

My fondest memory of her is of my early army days. I was activated at the University of Pennsylvania. On a weekend pass, I took Virginia home to Kit in Lancaster. Immediately I reported back to the university and in several days shipped out on a troop train to Indian Town Gap for indoctrination and assignment. As the train approached Lancaster, it slowed in the station but did not stop. I do not know how long she had been there, but there was my mother waving to me as the train rolled through the station. How she knew I was shipping I do not know, but I know she was on that train platform as we passed through Lancaster.

Growing Up McCaskey

We tried to live up to the McCaskeys before us in our household in Des Plaines. My father thought it was working. He wrote:

Two thousand years ago people predicted the end of the world and kindred disasters. They predict them today as well. Some years ago I stopped worrying about the world when the children interrupted my reading of "The Christmas Carol" to tell me that their committee had reached a decision. On Christmas morning, each child decided to pick out one of his gifts and take them to Maryville. Two thousand years is a long time. Quite a bit of Christmas spirit can build up in that time.

My parents wove a pattern of hard work and discipline into the lives of their children. They stitched this pattern with love.

My mother always found it amusing when someone asked her how much hired help she had. That was probably the reason my father nicknamed her "Laughing Girl." She did all the cooking and laundry and housework. The only real time she got a break was when she went into the hospital to have another baby.

During those refreshing interludes, Mrs. Passarelli took care of us. Instead of dinners of hamburgers or hot dogs, she prepared homemade pizza or spaghetti and meatballs. While waving a wooden spoon covered with meat sauce, she would yell, "You kids stop fighting." She never had to tell on us because my parents knew us very well.

There were many fights in our home and my parents used belts, fly swatters, spatulas, and pizza paddles as instruments of discipline. When my father's discipline was thought to be too severe, we buried one of his watches in the vegetable garden.

Our version of family planning was to have the children born during the Chicago Bears' off-seasons. We had seven victories and four ties. Six brothers eventually shared a bedroom. Each brother had two and a half drawers. Everyone carved his initials on his drawers, but there were many fights over the halves.

Education was very important in our home and chores were an essential part of our training. Grass had to be mowed and snow had to be shoveled. Dog pens had to be cleaned and vegetable gardens had to be cultivated.

My father was not a straw boss. He worked harder than any of his sons. When he cultivated a vegetable garden with a pitchfork and found one of his watches, he could appreciate the humor of the situation.

All of us were raised with discipline and love, and each of us was a special case. I started going to Bears' games when I was five. My brothers and I sat on an army blanket next to the Bears' bench while my grandfather coached. It was at one of the many games when we were present on the sidelines that he famously chided one official, "No man is completely worthless, you can always serve as a horrible example." This quote captures the wisdom and humor of George Halas—although he could be harsh, he was positive and encouraging.

At the McCaskey home of course, the intensity level came down when we were just "family." The best line that I've heard about family was from Father George Kane, who grew up with my uncle Mugs, George Halas Junior. On Wednesday, December 19, 1979, as part of his homily at Mugs's funeral, Father Kane said, "Family is where we take off our shoes, exhale who we are, and what we're about, where we're at our best and at our worst—where we can count on being understood and forgiven and loved."

Our Sons

For several years, I didn't want to coach my sons' teams because I coach them a lot at home. It's still a game of courtesy and grammar. I wanted them to get a different perspective. Besides, every time they did something right in a game, I'd want to call time out and shellac the ball.

However, when my sons were in seventh and eighth grades, I was one of their football coaches. I was an expert for a long time. Then I became a coach. Before most games, I said to my sons, "Good luck. Do your best because God doesn't grade on a curve. If you do your best, you're a winner, regardless of the score."

When my son, Ed, was in eighth grade, his team was in second place. When my son, Tom, was in eighth grade, his team made first place. When my son, James, was in eighth grade, his team earned first place.

My immediate family and I have been invited to Super Bowls and Pro Bowls. My wife, Gretchen, and I have declined because we wanted to keep our sons going in church, in school, and in sports. We used our vacation time to watch our sons play sports. My sons would play any position; they just wanted to play.

My goal as a parent has been to show interest without meddling. Any playing time is a great opportunity. I took notes at my sons' games. Taking notes at the games helped keep me quiet. Then I don't coach or officiate from the stands. This could be a problem for me. Once, I yelled at an official, "Jesus died for your sins." Note taking is much better.

My approach with my sons at games was that they were given this much playing time, and this is what they did with it. I provided accountability and encouragement. I showed my notes to my sons, but I didn't bother their coaches. All previous games were preparation for the next one. When my sons played, I considered their coaches to be great.

On Monday, September 29, 2003, the Bears played at the renovated Soldier Field for the first time. The Bears had begun their quest for a new stadium in 1956. Let the renovated stadium be a reminder: God performs miracles for people of faith who diligently work together.

Luxury Manor and Beyond

There is no perfect place on earth.
The Garden of Eden is closed.
Apple trees can be reminders.
I used to sleep with five brothers
in a bedroom called LuxuryManor.
Now I sleep with my wife.

A home in which there is love
Is an exciting place. How's marriage?
It's a wonderful life starring
Jimmy Stewart and Donna Reed.
I don't want any more trees in our yard.
Leaves fall during the football season.
Kids taking baths are good for laughs.
They are much shorter than giraffes.
For Halloween our kids are clowns.
Ducks on the pond can upturn frowns.
Geese on the shore are not a bore.
A fishing crane is not a snore.

When Gretchen is in repose,
Edward likes to count her toes.
While Thomas feasts on Gerber,
I enjoy reading Thurber.
Basement basketball is fun.
As a family, we've won.
I have no desire to roam.
I love to hang out at home.

—Patrick McCaskey

— Endnotes —

1   Noel "Paul" Stookey (of Peter, Paul and Mary), "Wedding Song," Public Domain Foundation, Wilder, Vermont, 1971.

2   Christian Community Development Association, *History of CCDA*, viewed at http://www.ccda.org/history (accessed October 27, 2010).

3   Wayne L. Gordon, *Real Hope in Chicago* (Grand Rapids, MI: Zondervan, 1995), 9.

4   Gordon, *Real Hope in Chicago,* 9.

5   Gordon, *Real Hope in Chicago,* 11.

6   St.Therese, the Little Flower, is famous for her simple childlike trust in God. She didn't see death as the end of her work for God. She looked forward to working after death in God's name. "After my death, I will let fall a shower of roses. I will spend my heaven doing good upon earth." St. Therese's "Little Way" was her philosophy that God is everywhere—in every situation and person—and in the ordinary, simple details of life.

QUARTERBACKING FOR NOTRE DAME HIGH SCHOOL

BEHIND ME, BEFORE ME, BESIDE ME

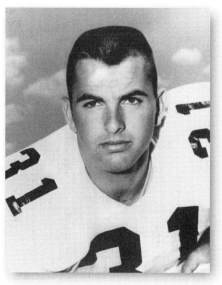

YOUNG BRIAN PICCOLO
AT WAKE FOREST UNIVERSITY

Football players wear protective gear, but no one who has watched the sport for long can doubt the risks players face on each play. In a game where 300-pound men move like missiles, the laws of physics play out in front of 60,000 plus fans in stadiums all over the United States.

In basketball, players routinely collide at impossible heights, then fall to the floor at every conceivable angle.

In baseball, the 90-mph fastball comes at a batter's head like a bullet. In horseracing, a diminutive athlete the size of a grade school gymnast rides on the back of a half-ton animal at blazing speeds. In hockey, players launch 90-mph frozen spheres through the rink, smash each other into the "boards" and as if that is not enough, they slash and swing sticks at every angle. Gymnasts fly through the air jumping off rings and bars doing flips that can literally be neck breaking. Figure skating, a sport that looks as graceful as ballet, can be deceptively dangerous for the athlete who practices a jump that propels the skater at an odd angle over the rock-hard ice thousands of times.

Athletes are courageous people. Courage is often needed both on and off the field of play.

SAYERS AND PICCOLO

When an athlete plays on a team, other athletes share the challenges and risks of the game. Teammates form close bonds that help improve their game and make for a stronger team performance. Many times, teammates help others face their fears with courage.

Bear players have formed some legendary bonds of friendship and fellowship over the team's history. Perhaps the most remarkable bond was that of Gale Sayers and Brian Piccolo.

Like many other teams, the Chicago Bears have seen their share of tragedy, but the one that comes to mind for most football fans is the tragic illness and death of Brian Piccolo. Brian Piccolo led the nation in rushing as a senior at Wake Forest in 1964 beating out his future teammate Gale Sayers. But at 5 foot 11 and 190 lbs., he wasn't very big; scouts also considered him too slow to draft. Nevertheless, he tried out for the Bears as a free agent and earned a position on the taxi[1] squad. In 1967, he saw increased action as backup to Gale Sayers, and the two became close friends when they became the first integrated roommates in the NFL. Piccolo took over for Sayers the following year when Sayers went down with a knee injury. He unselfishly supported and helped Sayers in his recovery.

When Sayers returned to play in 1969, Piccolo was once again relegated to the bench until he started in the backfield with Sayers. Then Brian developed a cough that led to medical tests and a diagnosis of lung cancer.

Christ Behind Me

As Piccolo was battling the disease, Sayers won the NFL rushing title and also received the George Halas Award as the league's most courageous player for the 1969 season. At the award ceremony, Sayers suggested that the most courageous player in the NFL was his roommate and friend Brian Piccolo who "has the mental attitude that makes me proud to have a friend who spells out the word *courage* 24 hours a day of his life....I love Brian Piccolo, and I'd like all of you to love him, too.

Tonight, when you hit your knees, please ask God to love him."

In the fall of 1969, I was home from college because of serious eye problems, which would eventually lead me to corneal transplants that would greatly help my eyesight. As a member of the Bears' family, my dad asked me to accompany the daughters of Brian and Joy Piccolo—Lori, Traci, and Kristi who were aged three, two, and one—to Atlanta to be with Joy's parents, while Joy herself flew to New York to be by Brian's side as he fought the disease.

Brian succumbed to lung cancer on June 16, 1970 and his life story and the Sayers–Piccolo friendship has been immortalized in the film *Brian's Song*. Brian's wife, Joy Piccolo O'Connell, is a crusader in the fight against cancer.

JOHN PERKINS

John Perkins is an inspiration to athletes and everyone who need courage. He is a black man whose early life was full of tragedy. He grew up just outside New Hebron, Mississippi where his parents were sharecroppers. His mother died while he was an infant and his father left the family to find work. In 1946, when John Perkins was in high school, his brother Clyde returned from the war as a decorated veteran. Clyde Perkins was attacked by a club-wielding deputy marshal who was spewing racial epitaphs at the young people who were waiting in line at the local theater. When the war veteran wrestled the club away from the deputy marshal, the lawman pulled a gun out and fatally shot Clyde.

John Perkins vowed to get out of Mississippi as soon as he could and never come back. Perkins left for California in 1947, where he went on a spiritual quest that led him to Christianity. He got married and started a family. He was ordained a Baptist minister in 1959.[2] His faith drew him back home to Mississippi, but without any specific evangelization plan.[3] Only after connecting with his community in Mendenhall, did he begin to orchestrate social and religious programs to counter racial hatred and debased conditions of minorities.

John Perkins was helping the people rebuild Mendenhall, Mississippi, the way that Nehemiah rebuilt the walls of Jerusalem. In the fifth century B.C., Nehemiah arrived in Jerusalem and rested for three days. Then he said, "'Let us be up and building.' And they undertook the good work with vigor" (Nehemiah 2:18b). Others caught the vision. Still others mocked the rebuilders. Nehemiah was prepared for mockery. He responded in a gentlemanly manner. After Nehemiah had analyzed the situation, he inspired others to join the project. He knew that God would provide the necessary strength. He also knew that his opposition wouldn't disappear. To set a good example for his people, he did not profit from the rebuilding of the walls.

Perkins began rebuilding Mendenhall with Bible studies and branched out. His ministries developed affordable housing and worked to have people develop a more worldly vision of their faith. The new outlook helped inspire the development of a thrift store, low-cost food for the poor, tutoring programs, and other initiatives. Perkins also noticed that as soon as young people graduated from high school, they moved away and did nothing to help Mendenhall. John encouraged indigenous leadership. He didn't want people with abilities, skills, and talents to leave. Some graduates stayed and others from outside the community were inspired to join in and help. Perkins's dedication to building up the entire social network would later earn him the nickname, "Father of Christian Community Development."

In the late 1960s and early 70s—an especially active period for civil rights—Perkins was severely beaten when he went to check on two of his associates who had been imprisoned. Recovering from being assaulted, Perkins moved to the state capital Jackson to expand his initiatives.

In 1982, after decades of service in Mississippi, the Perkins family moved to Pasadena, California, where Perkins and his wife founded yet another Christian community center. It established numerous programs for the poor: after-school tutoring, Bible studies, an award-winning technology center, summer day camp, youth internship programs, and a college scholarship program.

In 1983, Perkins established the John M. Perkins Foundation for Reconciliation & Development, Inc., to advance the principles of Christian community development and racial reconciliation throughout the world.

Perkins returned to Jackson in retirement in 1996, where he remains active in his ministries.

MIKE NEWTON

Mike Newton was a gifted athlete. In 1963, he began his athletic career at Notre Dame High School in Niles, Illinois. Out on the baseball diamond, he was the centerfielder. He was brought up to the varsity baseball team at the end of his freshman season. He was a three-year letterman in baseball, a two-year captain, and all-conference.

Mike played quarterback, halfback, and defensive back on the football team. In 1965 he was elected homecoming king.

After three years at quarterback, Mike was switched to halfback. In 1966, he had two rushing touchdowns, three receiving touchdowns (tied the single-game record), one kickoff return touchdown, and one interception return touchdown. He set the school record for kickoff return average (36.0). Mike attended Lakeland College in Wisconsin, graduating with a degree in sociology. At Lakeland, he was a four-year letterman in baseball, a two-year captain, and a two-year all-conference centerfielder. In football, he was a three-year letterman playing halfback.

When Mike was a junior, he met his wife, Jo, who was a freshman. Prior to their marriage two years later, she converted to Catholicism without Mike's prompting. Mike went to Illinois State for a masters degree in recreation. Jo went there as an art major. But they moved to Portland, Oregon a year later in 1972.

The Newtons settled in to raise a family in Portland. Mike enjoyed his work leasing cars, trucks, and equipment. Three sons were born: Pat in 1974, Chris in 1977, and Brian in 1980.

Mike learned discipline at Notre Dame, especially in athletics. Players had to be diligent or they wouldn't have played. When forced with hard times or stressful situations where an athlete needs to take action, rather than do nothing, the player does something and it works out. Even in defeat a player does not become discouraged. In team sports, people rely on each other and give it their all, not only for themselves, but for others.

Mike personified the most admirable athletic traits. He passed his sense of discipline and his penchant for action to his boys. Mike's sons were expected to be dedicated team players and on time for practices and meets. He put great stock in the importance of being a good father.

Mike is part of Notre Dame's Athletic Wall of Fame. He felt very humble and appreciative of the honor. He said, "It sets the tone for your children. If you are a hero to them, then you've really accomplished something. You've got to always be on your toes in front of your children."

Christ Before Me

Athletics were important to Mike, but the Newtons never lost sight of Christ. As Mike put it:

Religious training is very important. We pray together as a family and stress how the Lord is important. We show a lot of love at home. We attract people who want to know what we've got. We often minister to our friends and lay the foundation through example. We strive to be the best people we can be.

Mike could step back from a situation, analyze it, and then act accordingly with tact. He was never a forceful, stubborn person. He said, "You need to bend in a marriage and have patience. You've got to have tact. Lay the law down when you have to, but don't be combative or stubborn."

Mike always had a strong faith. He noted:

People can be so heavenly minded that they are no earthly good. You need to have balance and put things in perspective. You have to have compassion for other people. You shouldn't crowd people out of your life.

You live your life and then you die. What you've got left is the associations you've left. Try to leave something positive. Don't waste the precious time you're here. Most of the squabbles in families are over petty things.

Mike worked with his children so that they wouldn't have to misbehave in order to get the attention they needed.

He said, "The Lord doesn't steer a parked car. You need to pray on things, but don't use prayer as a copout for doing nothing. We're supposed to be growing, not dying. No matter what you believe, you can love your family."

I last saw Mike on Friday, October 6, 2006. He came to Notre Dame High School for the 40th anniversary celebration of the 1966 football team that was 9–0 and outscored opponents 341–80.

It's been said, "We know what people have been and, in a sense, what they have really done, only when we know how they died."[4]

In March 2007 Mike went to the doctor because of a throat problem, thinking he might have pneumonia. He was diagnosed with cancer of the esophagus and liver. It had spread throughout his body. He died on Friday, March 30, 2007. The funeral was Tuesday, April 3, 2007 in Oregon.

On the morning of his funeral, Jo called to tell me about Mike's death:

> As you probably heard, we lost our sweet Mike on Friday. It was incredibly peaceful. It was very, very fast. He was in very close touch with his heavenly Father and had had two lovely conversations very close to that time with his priest that he loved so much. The boys, the three of them and their wives, and some very dear friends were with us when Mike went. He went very, very peacefully.

He was a true champion and a warrior. Up until the very end, he was struggling to breathe for several days. He wasn't struggling exactly, but it was an effort to breathe. And he greeted, we figure, well over a hundred people that came to visit. Each one was with his arms opened wide for a hug and a few chosen, well chosen comments.

Always an "I love you," and "I'll see you soon," and "take care." Everyone who came to see him came away feeling uplifted. It was just an absolutely grace-filled time.

On Friday, October 21, 1966, Notre Dame played Saint Ed's at Notre Dame. Mike had 9 carries for 61 yards and 1 touchdown. He had 4 receptions for 79 yards and 3 touchdowns. He had 1 punt return for 6 yards. Notre Dame won 49–7.

I used to call Mike on October 21 and congratulate him. I won't be able to call him on October 21 anymore.

Everybody loved Mike Newton.

GOD'S STRENGTH TO PILOT ME

I was a normal Catholic boy. I wanted to play quarterback for the University of Notre Dame, which was named after God's mother. When I was a student at Notre Dame High School, Father Sandonato said to me, "McCaskey, you have a unique writing talent. You should develop it."

I replied, "Father, I have to get to practice."

In the spring of sophomore year, I was perhaps a little too intense and my classmates didn't seem to like me. I wanted to transfer. My parents would have allowed me to transfer, but first they wanted me to talk with my grandfather. He was not always a great listener, but he was that day.

After he had heard me out, he said, "This is a small test. If you run from this, you'll run when something really difficult happens later in your life. Those fellows are jealous of you because you have a lot of talent. So get in there and show them."

I followed his advice and stayed at Notre Dame. Things didn't get better right away. When I was a junior, I failed the football physical in the beginning of the year because of a hernia. I was out for a long time. I played quarterback for the last two plays of the last game. I handed off twice.

When I was a senior, I played linebacker, special teams, and quarterback. I knew what every position was supposed to do on every play.

Our team finished 9–0, outscored our opponents 341–80, and ranked as one of the top prep teams in the country. I was fortunate enough to be named to the "New World" all-American team as a quarterback. It turned out that Grandpa was right.

On the advice of University of Notre Dame Assistant Football Coach Joe Yonto, I enrolled at Cheshire Academy in Connecticut as a postgraduate to get another year of playing experience. Coach Yonto said that if I played well at Cheshire, then Notre Dame would seriously consider me for a scholarship. He also wrote a letter to Steve Kuk, the varsity football coach at Cheshire. To prepare for the 1967 Cheshire football team, I ran the district mile at Evanston High School in 4:37.9.

While playing catcher that summer, I had a lot of passed balls. When my father asked me why, I said, "I can't follow the ball." On August 28, 1967, my eye doctor, George Jessen, asked me how much my football career meant to me. I said, "It means a lot to me."

He asked, "Does it mean so much to you that you'd risk losing your sight?"

I replied, "No." After I got home, I quietly and slowly put my clippings and trophies in the garbage.

Kerataconus is an elongation of the cornea in the shape of a cone. I had what amounts to hernias of both corneas. So as a straight beam of light came into my eyes and bounced off the retinas, it came through the ripples wavy instead of straight. These distortions caused multiple or ghost images.

When wearing contact lenses, I could see 20/30, but it was hard to wear the lenses more than 12 to 14 hours a day because of the structural weaknesses of my corneas. There is a natural layer of tears between the contact lenses and the eyeballs. The tears filled in the ripples and the contact lenses acted like a glass bottom on a boat. Regular glasses were not helpful for my condition. In a letter dated August 31, 1967, Doctor Jessen wrote to my father:

> Dust, strain, and stress are the three most important things to avoid because when the eyelids squeeze the weakened tissue, they could cause it to stretch to the point of rupture. Therefore, football, baseball, basketball, weightlifting, or play or work in dusty surroundings are definitely contraindicated.

> The main thing in these conditions is the proper frame of mind of Pat and his family. Shed no tears, this may be a blessing in disguise. This is usually an affliction of the talented serious person who can and will make a worthwhile contribution to society for a long time…

My father said:

> The steel of manhood is tempered in the fire of adversity. Everybody has something wrong with them. Everyone's handicap is different because all of us are unique. When we are strong in an area in which others are weak, we are our brother's keeper.

Without contact lenses, I couldn't see clearly more than six inches. Binoculars magnified a television screen so much that it appeared as if it were six inches from me. So when I was unable to wear my contacts, I could watch television. I had been doing that since I discovered it by accident in 1969.

My grandfather told me how he started out in baseball, but he'd had to give up the sport because of a hip injury. It was only because of the baseball injury, he said, that he turned to football full time. He declared, "It doesn't matter what you do as long as you excel."

Thus, instead of playing football for Cheshire, I ran cross-country. I won most of my races, including the conference championship, set several records, and made all New England. Once again, Grandpa was right.

After the freshman cross-country season at Indiana University, I had to give up running for ten years because of eye problems. During that period, Doctor Halas kept after me to seek medical solutions. He urged me to remain optimistic and to persist in trying to improve myself.

I needed as much persistence as I could muster. Because of health problems, it took me six years to complete my undergraduate classwork. My last class at IU was Thursday, June 20, 1974. I started working for the Bears full time the following Monday. The players later went on strike.

I've been on the masters track circuit for people over 30 since 1979. In 1981, the Bears had a half-mile run to start training camp. One player, Kris Haines, finished ahead of me. He was later cut.

In 1982, I received a promotion. The Bears had a mile-and-a-half run to start training camp. After I finished first, Walter Payton said to me, "I tried to stay with you—then I said, 'That boy is crazy.'" That made all the training worthwhile. The players later went on strike.

On Thursday, July 25, 2001, I ran the National Masters 5000 meters race at Louisiana State University. I finished first in my age group. So I was a national champion.

My father kept after me to get corneal transplants. On Monday, April 7, 2003, Doctor Rubenstein gave me a right corneal transplant. On Monday, February 9, 2004, he gave me a left corneal transplant. I don't know who the donors were, but my father was the inspiration. I can see fine now without contact lenses, but I still can't play quarterback for the University of Notre Dame. I'm not bitter.

The Hebrew poet Yehuda Amichai expressed it, "The passing years have calmed me and brought healing to my heart and rest to my eyes."

— ENDNOTES —

1   Taxi squads are composed of players who are kept as reserves on teams for possible future play. Requirements are defined by league rules, their numbers are limited, and they are not counted as part of the active team players.

2   Jessica Kinnison, "Radical Faith: The Revolution of John Perkins," Jackson Free Press, December 17, 2008, viewed at http://www.jacksonfreepress.com/index.php/site/comments/radical_faith_the_revolution_of_john_perkins_121708/ (accessed October 27, 2010).

3   Randall Balmer, *Mine Eyes Have Seen the Glory* (New York: Oxford University Press, 1989), 178.

4   Sister Mary Faith Schuster, *The Meaning of the Mountain* (Baltimore: Helicon Press, 1963), 3

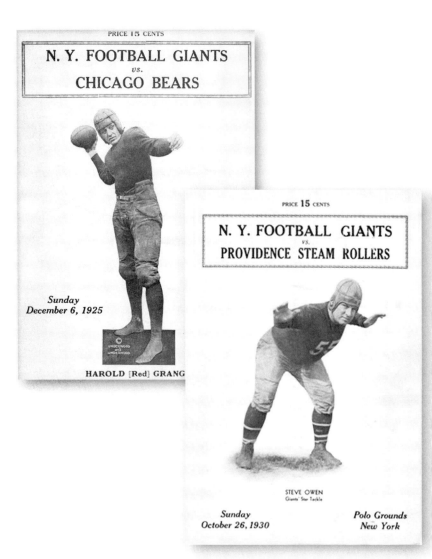

FOOTBALL PROGRAMS

EMPTY ME

VINCE LOMBARDI AT FORDHAM

It is only when you realize your nothingness, your emptiness, that God can fill you with himself.[1]

—Mother Teresa

You don't have to look very hard to see athletes smitten with themselves and all the material things that money can buy. Like all celebrities who constantly receive the adulation of strangers and friends, athletes can take a short jump into ego valley that must at some time be followed by a long climb to level ground. Sport requires that athletes pay a lot of attention to themselves—their training regimen, their diet, and their sleep. When they excel in their sport, who can blame them for thinking that they are special people? Well, they are. But being gifted and well conditioned doesn't make them better human beings. It is also natural for successful athletes to seek riches and all that comes with fame. But surrounding themselves with material treasure and noise leaves them no room for anyone else—not even for God.

Well Mara and the New York Giants

On August 14, 1916, Wellington "Well" Mara was born in New York City. On September 17, 1920, what is now the National Football League was born in Canton, Ohio. Well Mara's father Tim, an entrepreneur who was also a legal bookmaker, bought the rights to the professional football team in New York in 1925 for a reported $500. Mara's New York Giants—like other professional football teams—began and stayed on rocky financial footing for a long time, but the New York Giants won their first title in 1927.[2]

Tim Mara had many business interests. He gave Well and his brother Jack the New York Giants football team during the Depression in order to protect the team from potential creditors. [3]

Well Mara went to Loyola [High] School in Manhattan and Fordham University. In 1937 he went to work for the Giants. He served four years in the Navy during World War II.

Mara's Team

When Tim Mara bought the team, it had no name and no place to play. He modeled it after the baseball Giants by selecting the same name and negotiating a deal to play on their field during the off-season. Thus, the Giants football team originally played in the Polo Grounds, which was the hallowed ground of the legendary baseball Giants of John McGraw. Mara also wisely asked his savvy friend and fight promoter, Billy Gibson, to act as team president. Mara recruited Harry March who had football promotion experience as team secretary.[4] These men would help Mara fight an uphill battle to win fans in the baseball-crazy New York, home of baseball's Giants, Yankees, and Dodgers. On the field, at least, the Giants would be successful early and often.

Bob Folwell a successful college coach, was hired to manage the team. Folwell coached the Giants to 8–4 for the inaugural 1925 season, gaining the team a fourth place finish. They split with the Chicago Bears and the Providence Steam Roller, but took it on the chin, losing two to the Frankford Yellow Jackets. In 1926, they had a similar season at 8–4–1 under another coach, Doc Alexander. But in 1927—just their third year of existence—the Giants went 11–1–1. That record was good enough for the league championship under Earl Potteiger.[5]

In 1928, the Giants fell to a sixth place finish with a 4–7–2 mark, but rose right back again in 1929 with a 13–1–1 record for a second place finish under yet another new coach, Roy Andrews. In 1930, the team fought to a 13–4 finish for second.

1930s and 1940s

Steve Owens became head coach in 1931 and would stay in that position through the 1953 season. Two divisions were created in 1933, an East Division composed of the New York Giants, Brooklyn Dodgers, Boston Redskins, Philadelphia Eagles, and the Pittsburgh Pirates. The West included the Chicago Bears, Portsmouth Spartans, Green Bay Packers, Cincinnati Reds, and Chicago Cardinals.

After two fifth-place finishes, the Giants were Eastern Division leaders 1933 (11–3), but lost to the Bears in a dramatic league championship game 23–21. They were league champs in 1934 (8–5), beating the Chicago Bears 30–13 in an icy Championship game that would become famous as the "sneaker" game. Trailing 10–3 at half, the Giants changed to basketball shoes and their improved footing was largely given credit for the win. The field may have been the same for both teams, but the footing was not!

The Giants topped the Eastern Conference in 1935, but lost to Detroit in the league championship game 26–7.

Detroit was led by Hall of Famer Dutch Clark, who played tailback, and called the plays.

The Giants dropped to third in 1936 and climbed back up in 1937 when the team took second in the East. In 1938, atop the Eastern Conference again with an 8–2–1 record, the Giants beat the Packers in the championship 23–17. In 1939, the Packers returned the favor and beat the Giants in the league championship 27–0 after the Giants were conference champs once again.

After making it through the Depression, the Giants (like other professional football teams) faced another fight for survival during the 1940s war years as most players were inducted into the service and professional football attendance was low. In 1940, the Giants took third place with a 6–4–1 record, won the Eastern again in 1941 with an 8–3 record, but fell to the Bears in the championship game. A 5–5–1 record gave the Giants a third place finish in 1942. In 1943, it was the Washington Redskins who knocked the Giants off in the conference championship 28–0. The Packers defeated the Giants in the 1944 championship game 14–7 with the Giants setting an 8–1–1 mark for the season. The Giants had a poor season in 1945 with a 3–6–1 mark. The Bears would beat the Giants in the league championship game in 1946 by a score of 24–14 after the Giants had compiled a solid 7–3–1 finish in the regular season. A poor showing followed in 1947 when the Giants sank to 2–8–2.

It didn't get much better in 1948 when the Giants finished 4–8–0, but the season was noteworthy none the less.

That year the Giants signed the team's first black player: Emlen Tunnel. Tunnel was an exceptional athlete and man. He injured himself at the University of Toledo and then served in the Coast Guard in World War II. After the war, he enrolled at the University of Iowa, where he received attention from pro scouts. He left Iowa and showed up at the Giants' offices in New York uninvited. There he got a good look from the Giants staff, including Tim and Wellington Mara. Wellington said, "If you have enough guts to walk in here and ask for a job, I am going to give you a chance." He was signed and played safety for 11 years. He was an all pro defensive back and a gifted punt returner. He intercepted an incredible 74 passes in his 11 years with the Giants. He was also respected for his ability to defuse racial tension with good humor.[6]

As the decade closed in 1949, Ben Agajanian and Wellington Mara made football history. Agajanian was a college player in 1939 when his toes were sliced off in a freight elevator accident. His accident limited his play to kicking field goals and extra points, but he was very good at it. He shopped his skills around in the league and Wellington Mara was willing to take a chance on him. Mara allowed him to commute and show up on game days only. Agajanian was the first kicking specialist in football.[7]

1950s

The Giants would make the playoffs four times in the 1950s. Two coaching legends joined the Giants organization that decade: Vince Lombardi and Tom Landry. Lombardi came from West Point, where he had been an assistant coach. He was a former classmate of Wellington Mara at Fordham University, although they did not know each other while they were students. Landry came to the Giants in 1950 as a defensive back after spending a year with the All American Conference New York Yankees. Landry played two stints at the University of Texas: one before he went to war as a B-17 copilot and one after the war. Landry played fullback at Texas, but he had also seen action as defensive back and backup quarterback. Lombardi played line at Fordham and began coaching while attending law school. He decided not to pursue law. He taught and coached in high school before he entered the college game. By the time Lombardi was hired by the Giants, he was geared up for a head coach position.

In 1950, the Giants posted a 10–2 record, but the upstart Cleveland Browns won the division. The Giants began a series of personnel moves that would thrust the team into one of the elite of the decade. They drafted Kyle Rote in 1951, Frank Gifford in 1952, and Roosevelt Brown in 1953. Rote was a leader in the clubhouse. Future Hall of Famer Gifford could run, pass, and catch; he played halfback, defensive back, and eventually, flanker. Brown's Hall of Fame career would include 13 seasons at offensive tackle.

The Giants went 9–2–1 in 1951, 7–5 in 1952, and 3–9 in 1953. In a controversial move, Steve Owen was pressured to resign after the 1953 season. Owen was the consummate builder of teams and his creative work in both offensive and defensive formations and schemes was lauded. The Maras were remorseful over Owen's departure and offered him a scouting position.

The Giants were building and becoming a powerhouse. Assistant Coach Jim Howell got the nod as head coach, and immediately, Vince Lombardi was brought in to run the offense while Landry ran the defense. Howell wanted to oversee his team not manage the details. Under Howell and his young assistants, the Giants went 7–5 in 1954 and 6–5–1 in 1955. The Giants flexed their muscles in 1956, winning the division with an 8–3–1 record and playing the Bears in the championship game. The Giants annihilated the Bears 47–7 on an icy Yankee Stadium field, where the Giants once again (as in 1934) seemed to have the better shoes for the elements.

In the 1956 draft, the Giants added linebacker Sam Huff. With a solid defensive line including new acquisitions such as end Andy Robustelli and tackle Dick Modzelewski, the Giants were developing a formidable defensive force for the future. The Giants dropped down to 7–5 in 1957. In 1958 (9–3) and 1959 (10–2), the Giants won the conference but lost to the Baltimore Colts in two consecutive championship games.

1960s

In Howell's last year at the helm, the Giants notched a 6–4 season, good enough for third place in the conference.

Allie Sherman took over in 1961 and for three straight seasons, the Giants won their conference, but lost the championship game. Defeat came at the hands of the Packers in 1961 and 1962. The Bears beat the Giants in the 1963 match. Nevertheless, the Giants had been on an incredible run winning one league championship and five conference championships in eight years. For the next five seasons, the Giants played .500 or less. In 1969, Alex Webster took over for Sherman and posted a 6–8 record.

1970s

The 1970s would prove to be a challenging decade for the Giants. The team had a strong second-place finish in 1970, but neither Webster nor those who followed him could turn the program around. In 1974, Bill Arnsparger from Don Shula's staff joined the Giants and left in 1976 after a couple of losing seasons. John McVay took over and three more difficult seasons followed. The year 1979 would be a turning point for the franchise when George Young took over as general manager. The Giants hired Ray Perkins, who led the team to a 6–10 season to finish out the decade.

1980s

The 1980s would see a Giants Renaissance, but the decade started out slowly. Perkins's team finished out of the running in 1980 (4–12), but in 1981 started to climb out of that slump with a winning season (9–7). Momentum was lost in the 1982 strike-shortened season when they tallied a 4–5 record.

In the early 1980s, Young was quietly building a powerful team with excellent draft picks and the acquisition of other solid players. The Bill Parcells era began in earnest in 1983. Young had built a good team for the forceful Parcells to lead to greatness. From a fifth place 3–12–1 in 1983, Parcells's Giants would climb up to second in 1984 with a 9–7 mark. Returning to glory in 1985, the Giants scraped their way into the playoffs only to get run over by the mighty Chicago Bears.

In 1986, the Giants of Phil Simms, Lawrence Taylor, Mark Bavaro, Harry Carson, Jim Burt, Leonard Marshall, and Bill Parcells would not be denied. With a regular season mark of 14–2, the Giants marched through the playoffs and defeated the Denver Broncos 39–20 to win Super Bowl XXI. It was the storied franchise's first Super Bowl win. In 1987, the Giants finished fifth in the NFC East, but jumped right back up to a 10–6 mark the following year. In 1989, the Giants made the playoffs but were derailed by the Rams.

1990s and 2000s

In 1990, the Giants would win their way back to the Super Bowl, but it took a tremendous effort against the mighty San Francisco 49ers in the conference championship game. An equally inspired effort against the Buffalo Bills won them Super Bowl XXV in a 20–19 squeaker. Parcells retired and was replaced by Ray Handley. The Giants of 1991 (8–8) and 1992 (6–10) were not in contention.

Talented veteran coach Dan Reeves took the helm in 1993 and immediately the Giants improved to 11–5. After beating the Vikings in a wildcard game, the 49ers crushed the Giants in the division playoff. Reeves's Giants were 9–7 in 1994, 5–11 in 1995, and 6–10 in his final season with the team in 1996. Jim Fassel, a gifted offensive co-ordinator for the Arizona Cardinals, took over as Giants' coach in 1997. His 10–5–1 Giants lost a wildcard game to the Minnesota Vikings. After two mediocre years, 1998 (8–8) and 1999 (7–9), Fassal's Giants won the Conference Championship in 2000. The Baltimore Ravens clobbered the Giants 34–7 in Super Bowl XXXV. The organization settled back down to earth again with a 7–9 finish in 2001 and improved to a 10–6 in 2002. They sputtered to a 4–12 finish, in 2003.

Although his team started out slowly with a 6–10 season in 2004, new coach Tom Coughlin was the right prescription for the falling Giants. The 2005 Giants' 11–5 record got them into the wildcard game, but the team took it on the chin 23–0 against the Carolina Panthers. After a mediocre 8–8 season in 2006, the Giants won it all in 2007 having to go through the wildcard game in addition to the division and conference championships matches. In Super Bowl XLII, the Giants defeated the mighty New England Patriots of Tom Brady by a score of 17–14. In 2008, the Giants topped the NFC East, but were tripped up by the Eagles 20–14 in the divisional playoff match. An 8–8 record kept them out of the playoffs in 2009.

One constant through 68 years of the travails of one of the most storied franchises in all of sports was Well Mara. His Giants teams earned seven championships. They have done very well for an expansion team!

Mara's Family and Faith

Well Mara was so busy with the Giants that he didn't meet Ann Mumm, the woman who would become his wife, until 1953. They met at the back of a church when they rushed to help a lady who had fainted.

Well and Ann were married in 1954. They went to Mass every day. They said the rosary every day. They accepted children lovingly from God; they had 11. Each year at Christmas time, the parish confession schedule was hung on the refrigerator door with Well's handwritten note: No confession, no Santa.

After his children were married with children of their own, he would call to remind them about an upcoming holy day of obligation—attendance at Mass was required.

In 1981, I was interested in Well Mara's daughter, Susan. Well Mara wanted Walter Payton as compensation. So the deal fell through.

Well went to the Giants' games and practices and scouting meetings. When the Giants were on the road, after Mass, he called former Giants' coaches and players in those cities.

Well served on committees for many Catholic churches and hospitals and schools. Will Rogers said, "I never met a man I didn't like until two or more got together on a committee." Will Rogers never had the honor of serving on a committee with Well. Among his many charitable causes, he was especially committed to right-to-life causes like his Life Athletes organization that promotes chastity and respect for life with young people.

He went to his grandchildren's baptisms, first communions, graduations, Little League games, and school plays. He was never too full of himself to ignore others. He was humble and positive and supportive.

Well was inducted into the Pro Football Hall of Fame in 1997. He worked for the Giants for 68 years until he died on October 25, 2005, at the age of 89. He was inducted into the Sports Faith Hall of Fame in 2009.

New York—especially New York media—is known as a tough town for athletes and sports owners. Mara got his share of criticism from the press. Mara's friend Father George Rutler recalled a very personal attack. One sportswriter once wrote: "What can you expect from an Irishman named Wellington, whose father was a bookmaker?"

Mara's response, which he made to an audience at a kickoff luncheon, is perhaps one of the best quotations in sport:

I'll tell you what you can expect. You can expect anything he says or writes may be repeated aloud in your own home in front of your own children. You can believe that he was taught to love and respect all mankind, but to fear no man. And you can believe that his abiding ambitions were to pass on to his family the true richness of the inheritance he received from his father, the bookmaker: the knowledge and love and fear of God,...and second, to give you a Super Bowl winner.[8]

FATHER GEISZEL

A life is either all spiritual or not spiritual at all.
No man can serve two masters. Your life is shaped
by the end you live for. You are made in the image of
what you desire.

—Thomas Merton

Father Jack Geiszel grew up in Hollywood, California. During World War II, he was in the Signal Corps in the Pacific: New Guinea, Australia, and the Philippines. He noticed a difference in the attitudes of men who died. Those who had had religious training accepted death better. He came to the conclusion after being in the service that people needed religious help. Most thought he was too old to be a priest. The Jesuits took him.

The Bears used to stay in California for the entire week between the San Francisco 49ers game and the Los Angeles Rams game. Father Geiszel watched the Bears practice at Loyola High School. Many years later, he said Mass for the team one Sunday. The Gospel reading that day was the parable of the two sons in the vineyard. A father asked his sons to work. The first son said no, but did. The second son said yes, but didn't.

Father Geiszel spoke of effort, inspiration, and grace—how they can impact us when we are empty of our selfish concerns. Father Geiszel said there is "a pretty strong link between sports and spirituality. In sports, you have to put in a lot of time before you see results. The same holds true in the spiritual realm. The same qualities are demanded even though the immediate results are not apparent."

In his homily, Father Geiszel said:

This morning, the theme is that change through the grace of God is acceptable to Him. An orphan finished high school and went to Europe for a desolate life. He began to feel hollow. One night he had an insight. He tried to pray. The next morning he went to church. He felt peace. He decided to change.

He came back to the United States. He became a reporter for the New York Times. Then he became a Trappist monk. He was Thomas Merton.

The athletes here have had that same experience. You wanted to be athletes. Someone inspired you. You sacrificed and worked hard. The same thing happened to the Bears. You were on top for a long time. Last year you fell. Something got you going again. It might have been Mike Ditka. You're off to a good start.

The same thing can happen in your personal lives. You might have had a hollow feeling. Then a spark gets you going on the right path. It might be the readings today. The first son didn't want to work in the vineyard for his father. Then he reconsidered and worked hard.

Some people lead marvelous lives, but there is still room for improvement. We hope that everyone plays up to his potential today. With that will come good results. Let us reflect in thanksgiving for those who have helped us.

Papal Visit

Sports Faith International is a newly launched media initiative dedicated to using traditional and new media to showcase the connection between sports and faith. Catholic Athletes for Christ is a nonprofit organization established in response to Pope John Paul II's call to evangelize the world of sports.

Because of my work with Sports Faith International, I received a call from Ray McKenna, the founder and president of Catholic Athletes for Christ. Ray cordially invited me to help President George W. Bush and Mrs. Bush welcome His Holiness Pope Benedict XVI to the White House South Lawn on Wednesday, April 16, 2008.

First, I had to empty myself of my worldly concerns by emptying my calendar. I explained to my wife, Gretchen, that I might not be able to accompany her and her sisters, Lesley Conrad and Pam Bradley, as they drove to Asheville, North Carolina, for the funeral of their aunt. I explained to my son, Tom, I might not be able to be with his mother and his aunts when they visited him at Xavier University in Cincinnati on their way home from North Carolina. I explained to my son, Ed, I might not be able to see him pitch for Wheaton College on Tuesday, April 15, against Benedictine University of Lisle, Illinois. I explained to my son, James, I might not be able to see him play for the Loyola Academy sophomores on Wednesday, April 16, against Providence High School of New Lenox, Illinois.

They understood.

I arrived in Washington on Tuesday afternoon. I checked in at the Hilton Garden Inn, 815 14th Street NW. It is two blocks from the White House.

My son, Ed, pitched the first five innings against Benedictine University. He gave up one unearned run on three hits. He walked four and struck out one. He had one assist. Wheaton won 15–6.

On Wednesday morning, Ray McKenna and I walked to the White House. Then we stood for three and a half hours on the South Lawn with many thousands of other well-wishers. If it had rained, the event would have been cancelled, but the weather was perfect. The number on my ticket envelope was 10,159. People stood as far away as the Washington Monument and the Jefferson Memorial.

Making Room for Christ

All of us had made room in our own lives for the Vicar of Christ—we had emptied ourselves of our everyday lives and opened ourselves up for the message of Pope Benedict.

Kathleen Battle sang "Our Father." President Bush said, "Birthdays are spent with friends. We are honored that you are with us today on your birthday." The crowd sang "Happy Birthday" to the Pope.

President Bush said:

> Here in America you'll find a nation of prayer. Each day millions of our citizens approach our Maker on bended knee, seeking his grace and giving thanks for the many blessings he bestows upon us....

> Here in America you'll find a nation of compassion. Americans believe that the measure of a free society is how we treat the weakest and most vulnerable among us....

Here in America you'll find a nation that welcomes the role of faith in the public square. When our founders declared our nation's independence, they rested their case on an appeal to the "laws of nature, and of nature's God."

In a world where some treat life as something to be debased and discarded, we need your message that all human life is sacred and that "each of us is willed, each of us is loved" — and your message that "each of us is willed, each of us is loved, and each of us is necessary.…

Pope Benedict XVI said:

America's quest for freedom has been guided by the conviction that the principles governing political and social life are intimately linked to a moral order based on the dominion of God the Creator. The framers of this nation's founding documents drew upon this conviction when they proclaimed the "self-evident truth" that all men are created equal and endowed with inalienable rights grounded in the laws of nature and of nature's God. The course of American history demonstrates the difficulties, the struggles, and the great intellectual and moral resolve, which were demanded to shape a society which faithfully embodied these noble principles…

The preservation of freedom calls for the cultivation of virtue, self-discipline, sacrifice for the common good and a sense of responsibility towards the less fortunate. It also demands the courage to engage in civic life and to bring one's deepest beliefs and values to reasoned public debate...

The Church...is convinced that faith sheds new light on all things, and that the Gospel reveals the noble vocation and sublime destiny of every man and woman. Faith also gives us the strength to respond to our high calling, and the hope that inspires us to work for an ever more just and fraternal society.

After the welcoming ceremony, Ray and I walked to a Catholic bookstore that had a chapel in which we paid a visit.

Our next stop was the Catholic Leadership Institute luncheon at the Capital Hilton, 1001 16th Street NW. We were with Bishop Paprocki of Chicago. He plays hockey and is known as the holy goalie. We were also with Stan and Jill Mikita of the Chicago Blackhawks. After lunch, I tried to pay for the cab ride back to the Hilton Garden Inn, but Stan wouldn't let me.

My son, James, pitched the first 4.2 innings against Providence High School. He threw a hundred pitches. He gave up six runs on eight hits, one double. He walked five, hit two, and struck out two. He was 1–for–2 with a walk and 2 RBIs. Loyola tied 8–8. The game was called after seven innings because of darkness.

Thursday morning, April 17, Zed's Limo Service got me to Nationals Park for Mass with the Pope. There was a premium distribution of bags with *Catholic Digest, Magnificat,* Papal flags, and Mass booklets. I visited with John Hunt, the executive director of Legatus and a former lector at Saint Mary's Church in Lake Forest, Illinois.

I was in Lincoln Suite 10 on the third base side with Jim Murray, the former general manager of the Philadelphia Eagles, and his wife. The altar was in center field. Before Mass, the Procession of Bishops went from the first base side to center field. After Communion, Placido Domingo sang "Panis Angelicus."

In Pope Benedict's homily he stated:

In the exercise of my ministry as the Successor of Peter, I have come to America to confirm you, my brothers and sisters, in the faith of the Apostles. I have come to proclaim anew, as Peter proclaimed on the day of Pentecost, that Jesus Christ is Lord and Messiah, risen from the dead, seated in glory at the right hand of the Father, and established as judge of the living and the dead. I have come to repeat the Apostle's urgent call to conversion and the forgiveness of sins, and to implore from the Lord a new

outpouring of the Holy Spirit upon the Church
in this country.

After Mass, on his way off the field, the pope kissed
the baby of New York Jets quarterback Kellen Clemens.
The next morning I was at the National Catholic Prayer
Breakfast at the Hilton Washington Hotel, 1919 Connecti-
cut Avenue NW. I was at Table 42 with Kellen Clemens,
his wife, Nicole, their baby, Ray McKenna, Jim Murray,
Mike Piazza (a twelve-time Major League Baseball All-
Star), and his mother, Veronica.

President Bush addressed the multitudes while the
Pope was on his way to speak at the United Nations. The
president said, "I'm not used to being a warm up act. The
Chief Justice is here. He'll go anywhere to get a free breakfast. This is a great week for Catholics and not a bad week
for Methodists, either."

The whole experience was edifying, encouraging, ex-
hilarating, and inspirational. I feel more mellow and se-
rene. When I go about my usual duties, I feel smoother. I
also try to wave like the pope.

PAT WILLIAMS

Pat Williams was born May 3, 1940, and grew up in
Wilmington, Delaware, where he went to the Tower Hill
School. At the age of seven, he decided that he wanted
to become a catcher. He went to Wake Forest University

on a baseball scholarship. After he had graduated with a degree in physical education, he played for the Class A Miami Marlins. He also earned a masters degree in physical education from Indiana University.

Pat has worked for the Marlins, the Spartanburg, South Carolina Phillies, the Philadelphia 76ers, the Chicago Bulls, and the Atlanta Hawks. Now he is with the Orlando Magic. Pat was the original chairman of the Chicago Fellowship of Christian Athletes. He started the group in 1973.

Pat was the chapel speaker for the Bears prior to the game in Tampa with the Buccaneers on October 25, 1987. He talked about how he pursued monuments to man for the first 28 years of his life. He sought fortune, fame, power, and pleasure. He wanted to get rich, be famous, take control, and indulge himself.

Then he learned that Jesus Christ pardons sins. From the Bible, he found that the "peace of God passeth all understanding." He discovered a purpose for his life. He had a platform for witnessing through athletics. Regardless of what happened in the world, he could be triumphant. God's love is unconditional. Until our life is right with God, we cannot love.

Pat also talked about the three ingredients for a successful life: Have a self fit to live with; have a faith to live by, growing through a Bible study and a strong church (start in the book of James, where the rubber of life hits the road of reality, and let people build you up and hold you accountable); and have work to live for, letting God use you.

Pat was the main speaker at the Chicago Fellowship of Christian Athletes' 1988 Spring Banquet. FCA has meant a great deal in Pat's life. He was with a Philadelphia Phillies farm team when he became interested in Christian fellowship. He has gone on to touch many lives through the FCA.

For his banquet talk, Pat discussed Acts 18:24–28:

> Meanwhile, a Jew named Apollos, a native of Alexandria, came to Ephesus. He was a learned man, with a thorough knowledge of the Scriptures. He had been instructed in the way of the Lord, and he spoke with a great fervor and taught about Jesus accurately, though he knew only the baptism of John. He began to speak boldly in the synagogue. When Priscilla and Aquila heard, they invited him to their home and explained to him the way of God more adequately.

> When Apollos wanted to go to Achaia, the brothers encouraged him and wrote to the disciples there to welcome him. On arriving, he was a great help to those who by grace had believed.

Pat offered Apollos as a significant role model. Apollos was a man of strong convictions. He spoke boldly in the synagogue. He was willing to take a public stand, but his knowledge was incomplete. Two godly people began to teach him. He was willing to learn from others. He emptied himself of his ego and his pride so he could be filled with Christ and do His will.

Pat said:

> Lone wolf believers are not very effective. You need a support group.

> Apollos was an encourager. He had the heart of a servant. The world is not a playground. It is a battleground. Be a Christian encourager like Apollos. Tame your tongue. Use it for encouragement and uplifting. Encourage each other and stay behind for the injured until they are healed.

Pat appealed to the audience: "Have a teachable spirit. "Read devotionals and biographies and newspapers.…You should read the Bible every day. It was written over 1,500 years. We have to do the work. We have to read.…Young people need sound teachers. Be careful who you listen to." Pat and his wife, Ruth, are the parents of 19 children, 14 of whom are adopted from four foreign countries.[9] They emptied themselves of all their self interests to do the work of the Lord—to let Christ in their life.

When*

When I strive and thrive for excellence rather
Than rationalize mediocrity
And can realize I am no better than

Anyone else but certainly no worse,
When I know the sun will appear after an
Eclipse and know that apathy is the
Opposite of love and not hate, and not be
Self-centered so I listen to others,

When I can dream positively and think
Actively so that I can assist friends
Rather than handicap them and be grateful
To the good God for my natural gifts,
When I can have people take me earnestly
Through a feeling of duty and a sense
Of humor and yet be unique and make my
Presence felt without being obnoxious,

When I can maintain a belief in love and
Laughter rather than loneliness and tears,
When I stand in love rather than fall in it
And choose love gladly rather than madly,
When I can need someone because I love her
Rather than love someone since I need her,
When I have double cartwheels with only her
And have universal brotherly love,

When foes goad me into prudence rather than
Stupefy me into resignation,
When I am strong with faith in humanity
Rather than aggressive from fear of it,

When I can maintain a belief in "The Last
Flower" and "The Wild Flag" and also play
"The Trumpet of the Swan" to catch "The White Deer,"
Then I will have fully matured: all right.

—Patrick McCaskey

* With thanks to Rudyard Kipling for "If." The books mentioned in the
last stanza were written by two of the author's favorite writers: *The Last
Flower* (James Thurber), *The Wild Flag* (E. B. White), *The Trumpet of the
Swan* (E. B. White), and *The White Deer* (James Thurber).

— ENDNOTES —

1   Mother Teresa, *In the Heart of the World: Thoughts, Stories and Prayers* (Novato, CA: New World Library, 1997), 19.
2   New York Giants—Official Home, "*Team History*," viewed at http://www.giants.com (accessed on October 27, 2010).
3   New York Giants—Official Home, "*Team History*," viewed at http://www.giants.com (accessed on October 27, 2010).
4   Lew Freeman and Pat Summerall, *New York Giants: The Complete Illustrated History* (Minneapolis, MVP Books, 2009), 12–13.
5   Pro-Football-Reference.com, "1927 New York Giants," http://sandbox.pro-football-reference.com/teams/nyg/1927.htm, (accessed October 27, 2010).
6   Freeman and Summerall, *New York Giants: The Complete Illustrated History,* 54–55.
7   Freeman and Summerall, *New York Giants: The Complete Illustrated History,* 56–57.
8   Rev. George W. Rutler, "Wellington Mara," *Cloud of Witnesses: Dead People I Knew When They Were Alive* (New York: Scepter Publishers Inc., 2010): 71-73.
9   Orlando Magic—Official Home, *Orlando Magic Executives*, http://www.nba.com/magic/news/executives.html (accessed October 27, 2010).

WALLY HILGENBERG

ONE DAY AT A TIME

THE SKID ROW PRIEST—
FATHER IGNATIUS McDERMOTT

We think of athletes as being in superb shape. Training in the off-season with a personal trainer. We imagine them having a terrific workout ethic and watching what they eat. But that is not always the way it works. Athletes can often fall into the same traps as the rest of us.

Alcohol and drugs can be a problem. Often the battle on the field may be easier than the one that takes place off the field. Another aspect of sports and faith is evident when an athlete admits to problems and seeks help.

ANNY ABRAMOWICZ

Danny Abramowicz was born July 13, 1945, in Steubenville, Ohio. He attended Catholic Central High School there. Abramowicz was a three-year letterman at Xavier University in Cincinnati and is a member of the school's sports hall of fame.

In 1967, he was a 17th and final round draft choice of the expansion team, New Orleans Saints. Abramowicz did not have pro speed. At first it did not look like he was going to make the Saints. But Saints quarterback Billy Kilmer came to Danny's rescue in a preseason game against San Francisco by throwing to him at every opportunity. According to Kilmer, "He played so good they couldn't cut him."[1] Danny had the guts and determination to make the pros.

He played seven seasons for the New Orleans Saints. The team never won more than five games a season during that period. In his seven seasons at New Orleans he played wide receiver and special teams. He was an excellent player on a struggling team. In 1969 he was an All-Pro and led the league in receptions. Abramowicz stands third on the Saints' all-time list in receptions, touchdown catches, and yards.[2] He was traded to the 49ers and played for San Francisco in 1973 and 1974.

After football, Abramowicz became an analyst for Saints radio game broadcasts. He was also living in life's fast lane, becoming an alcoholic who was destroying himself and his family. He worked to repair his personal life and found he could only do that by restoring his spiritual life. Abramowicz thanks God for changing his life and allowing him to follow Him.[3]

In 1992, he returned to football as Bears' special teams coach through 1996. In 1997, when Mike Ditka moved to New Orleans, Abramowicz was hired as offensive coordinator. The Saints staff was fired in 1999 and Abramowicz retired from football.

Abramowicz credits the Holy Spirit with inspiring him to use his knowledge of sports and training to create a program on spiritual training that he espouses in speeches, on TV, and in his book, *Spiritual Workout of a Former Saint*. Abramawicz uses simple sports terminology to communicate his message. In 2008, Abramowicz began hosting "Crossing the Goal" on the Catholic television network EWTN. The program features a sports show format to encourage Catholic men to get into spiritual shape. Abramowicz is fighting what he calls spiritual atrophy.

Help Me Believe in What I Could Be

Dave Sims, the Louisiana Fellowship of Athletes Director, arranged for Danny to be the Bears' chapel speaker on Sunday, October 27, 1991. He was a reluctant substitute for his friend Archie Manning.

Danny said:

The Lord has done a lot in my life. Normally [Before], I was walking through a bar door. [Now] I teach at a high school here. The Lord put this Scripture on my heart to share with you, Hebrews 12:5-11.

…You have also forgotten the exhortation ad-dressed to you as sons:

My son, do not disdain the discipline of the Lord or lose heart when reproved by him; for whom the Lord loves, he disciplines; he scourges every son he acknowledges.

Endure your trials as discipline; God treats you as sons. For what son is there whom his father does not discipline? If you are without discipline, in which all have shared, you are not sons but bastards. Besides this, we have had our earthly fathers to discipline us, and we respected them. Should we not (then) submit all the more to the Father of spirits and live? They disciplined us for a short time as seemed right to them, but he does so for our benefit, in order that we may share his holiness. At the time, all discipline seems a cause not for joy but for pain, yet later it brings the peaceful fruit of righteousness to those who are trained by it."

In his talk, Danny went on to discuss his struggles in life and how scripture had helped him. He talked about his struggles as a player and how his small town background didn't prepare him for the challenges he would meet. His success in sports and business gave him a false sense of success in life. What he had really become was an alcoholic.

> In 1981, I entered Alcoholics Anonymous. I was angry and resentful. I became sober, but not serene. I had a desire to know more about the Lord. Finally, after a period of time, I came to realize that Jesus had to be number one. Booze and ego were number one. Jesus wanted me to do things for other people. The relationship with my wife improved, not by words, but by actions. The same with my children.

> … After I gave my life to the Lord, it got worse rather than better. I lost my mother-in-law, my mother, and my house. Finally, things started changing around. The Lord was changing me.

> … An opening came up at Jesuit High School. Coaching is a small part of it. When guys come into my office, about drugs, or divorce, or thinking about suicide, I can be there. There are a lot of people out there hurting. We have to make God number one in our lives.

Do it for God and not for men. You have to go through training camp. The Bears have to win by blocking and tackling. The Lord will train us. The Lord is with us. Now when I get in a bind, I turn to the Lord. I've never been so happy.

You can influence millions of people. When it's all said and done, God gave you the talents and your families. In order to be good examples, Jesus has to be number one. With Him, you do everything. Without Him, you can do nothing. Without Him, you'll always be aggravated.

I was the biggest sinner, the worst. If He can work in my life, He can work in yours. If the Lord had said to me, "Someday, you'll be leading the Bears' chapel service," I'd have said, "No way." He worked a miracle in me.

And All that I Am

After that chapel service, Danny had breakfast with Mike Ditka at the Bears' pregame meal. He made an impression and worked with Coach Ditka for several years. In addition to his television work, Danny speaks about his life in sports and faith across the country. His story is a powerful witness to faith. In 2008, he was inducted into the Sports Faith Hall of Fame.

Monsignor McDermott—
Apostle to the Addicted

The Chicago White Sox gained a future super fan on the 1909 Feast Day of Saint Ignatius, July 31, when Ignatius Daniel McDermott was born on the south side of Chicago.[4] He came from a large, nurturing Irish Catholic family.

Ignatius's father Michael was born in Ireland and moved from New York to Waukesha County, Wisconsin to Chicago. Michael settled in Chicago's Back of the Yards neighborhood and worked as a wagon maker. He decided to put one of those wagons to good use and started a milk delivery business. He bought milk cans from Indiana, pasteurized the milk in his basement, and then delivered the milk to his customers.[5] Michael married a neighbor, Ellen "Nellie" Bradley, whose ambitious family would share many political and religious interests with the McDermotts.

Nellie and Michael had eight children, with Ignatius serving as the caboose. Ignatius grew up on a mix of Back of the Yards grit, strong religious conviction, and Irish wit and humor. He was an enthusiastic sports fan who would follow the White Sox his entire life. The Chicago Cardinals originally had his allegiance in football, but eventually Ignatius would come around to the Bears.

Seminary

At an early age, Ignatius felt a strong calling to the religious life. He attended Visitation Grammar School, Quigley

Preparatory Seminary, and Saint Mary of the Lake Seminary in Mundelein, Illinois. He was an athletic young man, but his love of sports almost cost him his vocation.

George Cardinal Mundelein of the Chicago Archdiocese had built Saint Mary of the Lake Seminary. He was a progressive and a supporter of Franklin Roosevelt. The cardinal had a national reputation and he took a keen interest in his seminary's operation.

Nearing the end of his education at the seminary, Ignatius injured his knee badly during a scrub football game. Initial treatment did not help the stiffness that developed and he had to have surgery. The seminary's policy was that priests should be physically fit in every way to carry out their priestly duties.

The seminary's no-nonsense rector, Father Gerald Kealy, wanted to see the policy enforced and to toss Ignatius out. When some of the other faculty came to Ignatius's defense, he was given a reprieve. However, he had to spend an extra year in the seminary to make up class time missed due to his injury. The hobbled and disappointed seminarian would not graduate with the class with whom he had spent seven years. But his close call with expulsion made his vocation all the more precious to him.

Cardinal Mundelein got to know each seminarian well, and he and others sensed there was something special about Ignatius McDermott. The young man was popular among his peers and was known for his enthusiasm and his sense of humor. But he also had a compassionate heart.

During his seminary years, he worked one summer at Arlington Park Race Track. In order to board a train to the racetrack each day, he had to walk through Chicago's Skid Row. He was deeply touched by the plight of the addicted who lived there.

Father Mac

Ignatius was ordained April 18, 1936. Rather than send him to a parish, Cardinal Mundelein assigned him to Saint Mary's Training School (now Maryville Academy) in Des Plaines, which took in dependent children from kindergarten age through high school. The school had increased enrollments during the Depression due to the state of the economy. Many of the children had parents who were alcoholics, financially strapped, or ill. Many children had behavior or psychological problems themselves. McDermott struggled to understand the suffering: "Lord how come you shortchanged all these kids? And why was I given such a wonderful family and wonderful home?" McDermott would spend his life serving those who were in need the most—often, those who were overlooked by most everyone else. Wherever his vocation would take him, those around him came to call him Father Mac.

Blight of Alcoholism

Father Mac spent five years at Saint Mary's and he noticed a pattern in the broken homes that provided children for Maryville: At least one of the parents was an alcoholic.

Parental visits were spasmodic. He would visit them and find them drunk. Other parents would visit and be drunk. He began to get a first-hand understanding of the illness.

For the nonalcoholic member of the family and the children, Father McDermott suggested a formal program of support. He started a group for alcohol awareness on the third Sunday of each month. He knew people were thirsting for knowledge to keep the family alive. They were usually doing the wrong things. They were over-protective and denied the problem of alcoholism. He knew that alcoholics are very good manipulators and people would need help tackling the problem.

Father Mac served as an associate pastor at Our Lady of Peace Parish in Chicago from 1941 through 1946. He continued to see addiction problems as a parish priest. He saw firsthand that most alcoholics were not on skid rows; they were in everyday homes causing harm.

In 1946 Father Mac was named assistant director of the Chicago Archdiocese's Catholic Charities, which had an office 126 N. Des Plaines St. on the edge of Skid Row. Father Mac was frustrated by the seemingly ineffective treatment of the addicted—arrest and incarceration—30-day sentences, with the cycle repeating. He determined that alcoholism was a disease that needed treatment.

Mac's Ministry

Walking Skid Row each night, Father Mac would visit saloons and flophouses to gain the trust of the addicted, to offer help and encouragement. Father Mac had a personal ministry to alcoholics. He physically pulled them out of the gutter, prayed over them, and took them to hospitals and hotels. He followed their progress or lack of progress. He rescued them from attackers. He blessed them on their deathbeds. And at times, he was called to identify them in the morgue. He never gave up on them when everyone else had. He never gave up on them when they shouted at him and rejected his efforts, as they often did.

Some he remained in contact with for over 50 years. His ministry touched tens of thousands of families.

Father Mac earned his reputation as a selfless minister to the addicted. In time, he would use his name and influence to create a number of programs and ministries that would serve addicts and their families. Many of these initiatives are secular programs that are now publically funded. He founded the Central States Institute of Addiction (CSIA) in 1963. This program trains individuals, groups, associations, and professionals involved in handling addictions and assessments.

In 1963 he founded the McDermott Center for drug treatment. The center later became home to the Haymarket Center, which Father Mac and James W. West, MD, cofounded in 1975. Haymarket was the first free-standing, social-setting detoxification center in Illinois.[6] Haymarket continues to offer special treatment for chemically dependent people. It has expanded to offer programs to many others in need, including pregnant and postpartum women, drug impacted children, homeless men and women, HIV/AIDS sufferers, the mentally ill, and the elderly.

In 1979, Father Mac founded Intervention Instruction, Inc. (III) as a substance abuse education and prevention agency. It is one of the largest providers of rehabilitation education for Illinois residents convicted of driving under the influence of alcohol.

Show Me the Way

I went on a tour of the flophouses with Monsignor McDermott. One man told me, "Sixteen years ago, Father Mac gave me some money and told me to save it for a day. The next day I bought something to eat instead of something to drink. I have been sober for 16 years."

After I saw the McDermott Foundation on the corner of Washington and Sangamon in Chicago, I asked Father Mac to share the wisdom he has gleaned from over forty years of work with alcoholics:

> The alcoholic father is the passport to security. The alcoholic thinks, "Everyone has to change but me." When the paycheck disappears, it's either because of philandering, gambling, or drinking. Recovering alcoholics are the best counselors. We need to illuminate our minds and our hearts. Intervention and prevention are vital. Alcoholism is a physical, social, and mental sickness. Alcoholics shouldn't be punished.

Monsignor McDermott advised getting prevention programs into schools. Districts ought to find a tolerant teacher who would allow the subject to be taught, even in the grammar schools. In the late sixties and early seventies, Madison Street people would tell Father Mac, "If someone had told me in grammar school about the hazards of drinking, I wouldn't be here." The children of alcoholics become warped. They are overachievers or underachievers.

Sobriety and security are more enhanced in alcoholic company (a support group) that is a mixture or a cross-section of society. Priests should mix with laity in Alcoholics Anonymous meetings.

Monsignor McDermott said that we need to identify with the problem of alcoholism. Future addicts figure they will be social drinkers, but they believe drink will never control them and then it does.

Just how did Monsignor McDermott keep his head up all those years dealing such tough problems. "There is too much negativism in the world. Make a litany of positive things. The world thrives on encouragement. Understand a person with kindness—the only language the dumb can speak and the blind can see and the deaf can hear."

The man who was known as the "Apostle of the Alcoholics" and the "Skid Row Priest" died on December 31, 2004, at the age of 95.

WALLY HILGENBERG

Before the Bears played the Vikings in Minnesota on Sunday, December 3, 1989, Wally Hilgenberg was the Bears' chapel speaker. He had played football for the Iowa Hawkeyes from 1961 to 1963. As a senior, he was co-captain and All American. He played four seasons with the Detroit Lions and 12 with the Minnesota Vikings. He and his wife, Mary, had four children.

One of Wally's favorite Bible verses was Luke 15:10: "In the same way, I tell you, there is rejoicing in the presence of the angels of God over one sinner who repents."

As the Bears' chapel speaker before the game with the Vikings, Wally said:

My nephew (Jay Hilgenberg) plays for the Bears. I've converted to being a Bears' fan. I want you to know I understand this is a big game for you. I came to serve the Lord today. I understand where you are today. You won the Championship a few years ago. It's very hard to repeat.

After 16 years, it was difficult to retire from football. Two years before I retired, I accepted Christ as my Savior. Instead of watching cartoons on television before a road game, I flipped the channel changer and heard an evangelist. He talked about a free gift: the gift of salvation.

I wanted to get away from that. So I switched the channel and got another evangelist. He talked about how Jesus could be your best friend. When I was on the Vikings, I nicknamed myself Cheap Shot. I prided myself on how much I could drink.

I remember one year when we were trying to make the big push. I remember we were playing a Central division game. It was for the Championship. We went into the Old Met. People who were tailgating were encouraging me. It was a very hard game. We won the division title. The exit from the field was jammed. We heard everybody cheering for us.

After we had finally cleared the field, instead of signing autographs and bumming a few Scotches from tailgaters, I went back inside the stadium. It was very cold and empty, just like my life. I turned to my wife, and she said, "What's missing in your life is Jesus Christ."

The next week was a road game. I read the Gideon Bible. I was a biblical illiterate. God was calling me to make a commitment in my life. My Dad got saved at the kitchen table when he was 78. I invited Jesus into my life as Lord and Savior. I pledged to serve Him for the rest of my life.

The Bible talks about the victorious, abundant life. I went to chapel service for the first time. I tried to sneak in the back. Jeff Siemon thanked me for coming to chapel service. Two years previous[ly], he and Fred Cox had picked out the least likely guy to become a Christian. It was me. They had been praying for me for two years. My wife had been praying for me for six months.

After I made the commitment, things started happening in my life. The Lord began to take that pride out of my life. When my son asks me about my day, I can honestly tell him if I'd had a bad one. Then he prays for me.

I had the most violent temper, you'd ever seen. I never knew peace until I knew Jesus. It doesn't take away from being a football player. It adds to it.

My wife had a propaganda campaign. She left tracts around the house. I used to say, if I ever became a Christian, I wouldn't give up drinking. Two months after I accepted Christ, alcohol tasted poorly. I stopped drinking.

You guys have a big game today. Play for the Lord's glory, not your own. Victory in Jesus is forever. I can't think of another football team I'd like to play for than the Chicago Bears. The Lord's team is even greater.

Ginger ale

Three generations of my family were alcoholics until my father put it on hold. When he was fifteen, he had five beers while singing in a saloon one night. His head was spinning. He came home and said to his mother, "I'll never drink again." He never did.

When I was growing up, I heard that story quite often. It seems that those who indulge in the practice of becoming inebriated end up having to do so quite regularly. My father warned me to stay away from this practice because he had seen the tragedy it had brought three generations.

As one of eleven children, I rarely had any so-called soft drinks in my youth. They were considered luxury items.

When I went off to college, I didn't want my peers to label me a deviant. So I carefully took notes on the actions of my peers throughout the first semester.

During the second semester, it was my turn to make a run to the liquor store. I left the old suitcase for the old suitcase trick out in the car. Then I went inside and asked for a case of ginger-ale. Luckily, the storekeeper didn't ask for my driver's license. I brought the ginger ale out to the car and loaded it into the suitcase.

When I got back to the dorm, I tried to act as inconspicuous as possible. It admittedly was difficult because it was my first run and I was quite nervous. There were no campus police around and I made it up to my floor without incident. The guys greeted me joyously and locked the door hurriedly behind me. I put a towel under the door and turned the fan on to blow outward so all of the fumes would blow out of the room.

When my peers discovered the ginger ale, they acted as if they were not upset, but they never forgot about my caper. A year later, they helped me celebrate my twenty-first birthday.

After dinner in the cafeteria, I was suddenly very popular—or at least there was a group of guys who were surrounding me. They chased me on foot over much of the campus. Finally, a posse in a car caught me. Then they brought me back to the dorm and threw me into a bathtub of ice water. They also held me upside down in the men's urinal while they flushed it. These are known as a tub and a swirlie. Peer pressure is powerful!

When my wife and I got married, we served no alcohol at the reception. We had a wonderful celebration that was a lot of fun without it. We served ginger ale.

Neither of us even drinks coffee. The table in our living room is known as the milk table. When we have guests in our home, instead of marijuana, we pass around our wedding book. I am sober and my father is a hero. The world is a better place because I don't drink alcohol.

— ENDNOTES —

1   Bill Lubinger, "Who dat? Danny Abramowicz Was the New Orleans Saints' First star, and Will Root for His Old Team from his Steubenville Home," *The Plain Dealer,* January 31, 2010, viewed at www.cleveland. com/sports/index.ssf/2010/01/who_dat_danny_abramowicz_was_ t.html (accessed October 27, 2010).

2   Bill Lubinger, "Who dat? Danny Abramowicz."

3   Danny Abramowicz*, Spiritual Workout of a Former Saint* (Huntington, IN: Our Sunday Visitor Publishing Division, 2004), 10.

4   Thomas F. Roesner, *Father Mac: The Life and Times of Ignatius D. McDermott, Co-Founder of Chicago's Famed Haymarket Center* (Chicago: McDermott Foundation, 2002), 23.

5   Roesner, *Father Mac: The Life and Times of Ignatius D. McDermott, Co-Founder of Chicago's Famed Haymarket Center,* 32.

6   Haymarket Center—Official Home, *"The Life of Father Mac,"* http:// www.hcenter.org/about us/maclife.html (accessed October 27, 2010).

PAPA BEAR—BETTER TO KICK THAN TO RECEIVE

SIMPLE GIFTS

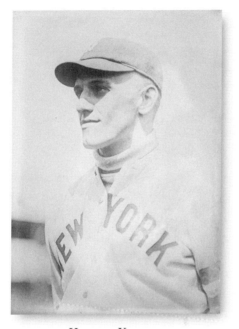

HALAS AS YANKEE

The Shaker hymn, "Simple Gifts," is a plain, but powerful hymn. Its lyrics and tune are credited to Joseph Brachet at the Shaker community in Alfred, Maine, in 1848. Aaron Copland used it in his *Appalachian Spring* ballet and orchestral suite.[1] Copland's composition captures the essence of our simple American piety that grows powerful when we find our place in the glory of creation. The lyrics advocate that we keep "turning" or moving as in dance until "we come round right."

"Simple Gifts"

'Tis the gift to be simple, 'tis the gift to be free,
'Tis the gift to come down where we ought to be,
And when we find ourselves in the place just right,
'Twill be in the valley of love and delight.

When true simplicity is gain'd,
To bow and to bend we shan't be asham'd,
To turn, turn will be our delight,
Till by turning, turning we come round right.

Our country's early settlers often talked about the role of Providence or divine guidance in our nation and our lives. We seek and, with the grace of God, we find. Many successful people have a multitude of talents, but they also have a burning desire to do exactly what they are called to do. Often, talented people pass up many opportunities along the way that most people would have held tight. They want to get to just the right place for them. Often this path is especially difficult for athletes and coaches who have many choices. Ray Meyer had to say goodbye to Notre Dame before he began his long successful career at DePaul. Vince Lombardi left the Giants on his way to Green Bay. Tom Landry left the same Giants on his way to the Cowboys. George

Halas said goodbye to the New York Yankees before he decided on a career in football. It is a gift to end up where you ought to be.

GEORGE HALAS

George Halas is a larger-than-life figure for many sports fans. He was also my grandfather, godfather, and founder of the family-owned business—the Bears. Although his life was hard, it was fantastic on so many levels. His life's story is a living history of 20th Century America. Stamped upon his character are lessons from the Great Depression, World War I, and World War II. In so many ways, his life was successful because he had faith, worked hard, and never gave up. He saw problems as opportunities. He moved on from setbacks at lightning speed.

Born in 1895, he came from hardworking parents. Frank and Barbara Halas had eight children, with four surviving to adulthood. Frank was a tailor. He and Barbara scraped together enough to buy a three-story building in Chicago. Barbara ran a grocery store on the first floor.

While George was in high school, his father died, but his industrious mother carried on. She eventually sold their building and moved into an apartment where she opened a tavern in the living room. She wanted her boys to get a college education.

Although tall and thin, George Halas was as tough as nails and loved to play rough. He was a gifted athlete, but not as gifted as some of his contemporaries, such as Babe Ruth, Jim Thorpe, and Red Grange—all of whom played a role in his life.

Halas played baseball and lightweight football and set many records in track and field at Crane Tech in Chicago. After high school, he worked for a year at Western Electric in Cicero, Illinois, before starting college and he came back to the industrial giant each summer. He attended the University of Illinois with his older brother Walter, who was the Illini's star pitcher.

University of Illinois

George Halas had a lot of heart, and although he was a thin underclassman, he started out with designs at playing the halfback position. He took a terrific beating. He switched over to end and impressed coach Robert Zuppke in subsequent years. Halas broke his jaw diving for a tackle in the days before players wore facemasks.[2] He was so tough he broke his leg and continued to practice, attempting to ignore the pain until the coach criticized his play. After a five-day hospital stay, he was back on the sidelines to cheer his team on in practice.[3] He made a name for himself at the university and established friendships there that would last a lifetime.

Coach Zuppke is a legend at the university, where he won induction into the College Hall of Fame on the strength of a 28-year career for the Illini during which his team won four national championships.[4]

On the basketball court, George Halas played for Ralph Jones, another remarkable coach. Jones was an excellent teacher and very versatile. In addition to basketball, he coached baseball and football. Halas had a physical intensity on the court that the coach had to help him control. Halas liked Jones so much that he would later ask him to coach the Bears.

Halas played baseball under yet another University of Illinois legend, George Huff, who had also coached football and served as athletic director. Like his brother Walter, George Halas was an excellent college baseball player. He enjoyed baseball most of all.

As an upperclassman, George Halas had done well in football. The speedy end was also returning kickoffs and punts. He had performed well on the baseball team, playing outfield and batting about .350. In his senior year in the midst of the basketball season, the United States entered World War I.

World War I Service

Anxious to serve his country, with only six credit hours remaining to graduate, Halas joined the Navy. The university granted him a degree and sent his diploma on to the family after he left for war. He entered Officer Candidate School and ended up serving at Great Lakes Training School as recreation officer. A far cry from the sea duty he had envisioned, but it was a providential assignment that brought him together with a "who's who" of great college players. The Great Lakes football team was a powerhouse in 1918.[5] This second "college career" gave Halas another opportunity to shine and play with a terrific group of athletes. It also provided an opportunity to size up the best talent in football for the future.

Yankees

Halas also played baseball at Great Lakes and must have made an impression on the diamond. After the war ended, he was invited to the Yankees' spring training. He was an excellent outfielder, but he had difficulty hitting the curve ball—a malady that has ended many a professional baseball career. But because he showed so much promise in the field and was a switch-hitter, Yankee manager Miller Huggins kept him on. A hip injury threatened his career early, but his condition improved after treatment by the famous hands of "Doctor" Bonesetter Reese of Youngstown.[6] Halas got right back to work. Unfortunately, he continued to have difficulties hitting and he was sent down to St. Paul for more seasoning. He was making good progress, but not quick enough for his high expectations. The Yankees were acquiring a young man named Babe Ruth and they had plenty of veteran talent on the team. They simply did not have room for a player who needed more time to develop. When Halas was asked to return to the minors for one more season, he declined.

Back to Football

After starting a new job working for the Burlington and Quincy Railroad, Halas tried out and made a semipro football team, the Hammond Pros. In his first game, he saw celebrated athlete Jim Thorpe and Hammond team-mate Gil Falcon repeatedly go after each other like a couple of charging bulls. Thorpe ended up winning the game on a touchdown run that was followed by a fine play on defense. George Halas was impressed with how football could attract a crowd, even at a semipro level.[7] He must have also been impressed by how men who were past their college years could get bigger, stronger, faster, and tougher—taking the sport to a new level. Thorpe was a one-man sports franchise who might play on several different teams in a single week.

Halas was recruited to work at Staley Starch Company in Decatur in a dual management training and athletic director position. Staley had baseball, basketball, and football teams. Halas cut his management teeth running the Staleys. Halas sensed an opportunity to organize the teams that had been playing together to form a league. A letter to Canton Ohio's Ralph Hay got things rolling. Hay invited the interested parties to Canton, where they outlined the basic league structure. The Staleys and 10 other teams pitched in $100 each and made up the new American Professional Football Association that would eventually morph into the National Football League. Among the team managers was Jim Thorpe. Like early professional baseball, professional football would be a precarious business investment.

On October 3, 1920, George Halas won his first game as coach of the Decatur Staleys against the Moline Tractors.[8] Halas would play in 12 games that season and catch two touchdown passes.

In 1921, the economy hit a downturn. The Staley Starch Company determined that it could no longer afford the team. Owner A. E. Staley seeded some funds to Halas that allowed him to start up his own team in Chicago.[9] Halas made fellow University of Illinois alum, Edward "Dutch" Sternaman, whom he had recruited in 1919, co-owner. Of the original 11 professional football teams, only two would survive: The Decatur Staleys and the Racine (later Chicago, still later, Arizona) Cardinals.

By Turning, Turning, We Come Out Right

Faith can lead us to that "place just right." Those who keep that faith, keep "turning until they get there." Hope and faith kept George Halas going in the face of great adversity. Faith held him on the right path.

Halas's "place just right" was Chicago, where he moved the Staleys and worked with Chicago Cubs President William Veeck Sr. to arrange playing time in Wrigley Field. Halas was a baseball fan and originally wanted to call his team the Cubs. Later, he settled on the Bears, given the larger size of football players. The Racine Cardinals were a team with roots along Racine Avenue on the south side of Chicago.

Having a great deal of experience with players of the era, he had an eye for talent, understood the player's mentality, and worked diligently to establish professional football.

For many years, professional football was a financially fragile undertaking. Players were paid on a game-by-game basis and sometimes the money was difficult to find. A poorly attended game could be financially disastrous.

Early Bears in the 1920s

In the early 1920s, the Bears and professional football struggled in obscurity, but Halas kept faith that the team and the game would prevail. In 1921, the Bears would play as the Chicago Staleys. They would win the league championship on the strength of a 9–1–1 record. It would also be the year an independent professional club, the Green Bay Packers, would join the league.

In 1923, the Bears played Jim Thorpe's Native American team from LaRue, Ohio. Halas picked up a Thorpe fumble on the two-yard line and ran it back 98 yards for a touchdown.

As Halas struggled to keep the Bears going, he was contacted by C. C. Pyle who was positioning himself as agent for University of Illinois football sensation Red Grange. Grange was not just a great football player; he was the best ever for a short time. Moreover, he was certainly one of the most entertaining sports figures to ever put on a pair of cleats. He was so difficult to tackle, Chica-

RED GRANGE—THE WHEATON ICE MAN WITH ADMIRERS

go sports writer Warren Brown called him the "Galloping Ghost." He was especially famous for long, fan-pleasing runs. In 1924 against a University of Michigan team that had a long winning streak, he ran back the opening kickoff 95 yards. The Galloping Ghost scored five touchdowns for the day and passed for another score. He gained 402 yards in that one contest including 212 rushing, 64 passing, and 125 on kickoffs. Grange was three-time All American and made the cover of *Time Magazine*. His number 77 at the University of Illinois was retired in 1925. That distinguished honor has only been given to one other player in University of Illinois history: Dick Butkus, number 50, was retired in 1986.

Pyle suggested to George Halas that Grange could draw huge crowds for the Bears, but he would need a large stake in the gate receipts in order to play ball. Halas agreed to pay Grange handsomely for his efforts. The Bears went on an exhausting barnstorming tour late in 1925 into early 1926. The crowds and the gates were large. The tour not only helped improve the Bears' financial footing, it improved team finances in other cities where Grange played. It was never easy to keep the Bears running and it took decades for the franchise to make a consistent and comfortable profit. Persistence and grit made it happen. Only those as tough as George Halas could make it.

For many Americans, college football was the best kind. Some feared professional football would ruin the sport. But Halas and others were convinced that professional football could be more entertaining than the college game because athletes would continue to improve and develop after college. In early 1926, in order to quell fears in the college ranks and improve the reputation of professional football, Halas and the league established a rule that young men could not be signed to the professional ranks until after their college class had graduated.

After the Bears' barnstorming tour, the ambitious Pyle took Red Grange and started up his own professional football league. His American Football League folded in a year. His team, the New York Yankees, moved over to the National Football League with Red Grange in tow, but it did not survive. After a few years with the New York Yankees football team while it was part of the American Football League, Grange had to sit out all of 1928 with a knee injury. He would return to the Bears in 1929, but his injury had taken its toll. Grange was never the "Galloping Ghost" again, but he was an excellent defensive back for the Bears.

The Bears would win no more championships in the 1920s. Halas's own playing career wound down and ended on December 15, 1929. Having played in the days of leather helmets, Halas had broken his jaw and his leg—he knew what the sport demanded. His decade playing for the Bears naturally earned him a unique respect among players and coaches. He played his last professional game as the Great Depression was taking hold of the country.

Papa's Bears in the 1930s

In 1930, George Halas and co-owner Dutch Sternaman hired Ralph Jones, who was at Lake Forest Academy, to coach the Bears. They both knew Jones from his days at the University of Illinois. Jones made innovative adjustments to the Bears' offense that gave the team a more mobile attack. Adding University of Minnesota standout, Bronko Nagurski, gave the Bears one of the greatest power-runners of all time as well as a bone-crushing tackler. With Red Grange and several other excellent players on the roster as well, the Bears were a formidable power. They won the league championship two years running: 1932 and 1933.

However, the Bears were almost derailed in 1931. Sternaman needed money and decided to sell his stake in the team. Tough negotiations between the two partners were followed by some desperate financial moves by Halas to raise the money at a time when many of the banks had gone out of business. A few good friends and some last-minute maneuvers saved Halas's stake in the Bears.

In 1932, Chicago and Portsmouth led the league with identical 6–1–6 records after the last scheduled game of the season. It was determined that a championship game would be played in Chicago. Horrific weather sent the teams indoors to the Chicago Stadium, where the game was played on an abbreviated field. The Bears triumphed in a 9–0 game that featured a Nagurski to Grange touchdown pass and a safety.

Jones left the Bears to become athletic director at Lake Forest College. George Halas became sole head coach of the Bears in 1933. He served in that capacity for most of the next 35 years. Two league conferences were created in 1933. An East Conference included the New York Giants, Brooklyn Dodgers, Boston Redskins, Philadelphia Eagles and the Pittsburgh Pirates. The West was composed of the Chicago Bears, Portsmouth Spartans, Green Bay Packers, Cincinnati Reds, and Chicago Cardinals. The conferences would allow the leaders from each to battle for the title in a championship game. With Halas at the helm, the Bears beat the Giants in the first scheduled championship game 23–21 to win top honors in 1933.

The Bears looked unbeatable in 1934, when they went 13–0 for the season. They had won 18 straight games and were dominating the league. The championship game was one for the history books. On icy field conditions, the Bears took a 10–3 lead into the half. During the break, the Giants changed from cleats to sneakers that their equipment manager had borrowed from Manhattan College. The new shoes allowed the Giants to outmaneuver the Bears and the sneakered team scored 27 unanswered points for a 30–13 win. The game is called the "Sneaker Game."

After a few tough seasons, the Bears roared back in 1937, winning the Western Conference. In the league championship game they played the Eastern Conference

Champions, Washington Redskins. The Redskins had moved from Boston after poor attendance created huge financial losses. Washington won the game 28–21 on the strength of a spectacular performance by quarterback Sammy Baugh. Future Hall of Famer Baugh threw three touchdowns in the third quarter, including two long bombs of 55 and 78 yards to another future Hall of Famer, Wayne Millner.

Bears in the War Years

In sports, teams have peaks and valleys. As the 40s approached, Halas began "retooling" by acquiring new players and planning a new offense. The coach was looking for someone very bright to run a new, more complex offense that he had developed with help from University of Chicago's Clark Shaughnessy. Halas snagged heady Columbia University quarterback, Sid Luckman, in the 1939 draft for that role. He also added Bill Osmanski in the same year. Clyde "Bulldog" Turner and George McAfee were acquired in 1940 prior to the season. With a powerful lineup and new offense, the Bears were commanding, but not invincible. During the season they were 8–3, good enough to win the Western Conference and battle the Washington Redskins for the championship. The Bears clobbered the Redskins 73–0, the highest score in NFL history.

In 1941, the Bears were 10–1, tied with Green Bay in their division. The Bears beat the Packers 33–14 in a game that featured an 81-yard punt return by Hugh Gallarneau and George McAfee's terrific 119-yard rushing performance. The Bears went on to beat the Giants in the championship game for the Bears' second title in a row.

As the 1941 season was closing, the Japanese bombed Pearl Harbor and the United States became a combatant in World War II. Halas wanted to contribute more actively to the war effort than his assignment had allowed him in World War I. After he coached his near-perfect Bears to their first five wins in 1942, he left for duty in the Naval station in Norman, Oklahoma, and then on to the South Pacific. In the South Pacific, Commander Halas, USNR, used his considerable organizational, persuasive, and leadership talents to serve as recreational and welfare officer of Admiral Thomas Kincaid Seventh Fleet. Kincaid supported McArthur's command and the commander was kept pretty busy.

At season's end, the 11–0 Bears took on the Washington Redskins again for the championship. This time the Redskins prevailed 14–6.

The 1943 Bears would play without George Halas as the war continued. The league suffered financially and players were in short supply. Assistants Hunk Anderson and Luke Johnsos coached the Bears to another great season. They were helped immeasurably when Bronko Nagurski was coaxed out of retirement after leaving football in 1937. Nagurski had become a legendary wrestler after leaving football. Nagurski at 6-foot-2, 235 pounds, had the size to play fullback today and the heart to play it in any era. In his first professional football stretch, he played fullback and defensive line. When he came back to the Bears, he played tackle. When the Bears were trailing the Cardinals in a must-win game at the end of the season, Bronko returned to his fullback position, scoring a key touchdown and turning the tide in favor of the Bears. He returned again as fullback in the championship game in which the Bears beat the Washington Redskins 41–21.

The Bears dropped down in the standings in 1944 and 1945, but came back strong at war's end as their premier players and Coach Halas returned from war. In 1946, the Bears racked up an 8–2–1 record. They beat the New York Giants in the title game 24–14. The Bears could look back at one of the most remarkable runs in sports history: four championships in seven seasons.

In 1948, the Bears signed legendary Notre Dame lineman, George Connor. Connor originally went to Holy Cross, served during the war, and then played for Notre Dame. The Fighting Irish won two consecutive national championships with Connor and another future Bear, Johnny Lujack.

To stop a powerful Eagles running attack, Connor who was agile and fast although 6-foot-3 and 240 pounds, moved to linebacker. His success there helped establish a larger prototype of player in that position.

For the remainder of the 1940s and throughout the 1950s, the Bears built a reputation as one of the toughest football teams, but the organization would not see another league championship season until the 1960s.

Bears in the 1950s and 1960s

In 1956, Halas turned head coaching duties over to Paddy Driscoll. Driscoll coached the 1956 Bears to a 9–2–1 record that led the Western Conference. They met the New York Giants in the championship and took it on the chin 47–7. The Bears slipped to under .500 in 1957, and Halas returned to coaching in 1958.

In the late 50s, the Bears were rebuilding. Johnny Morris and Abe Gibron came along. Linebacker Larry Morris, who had played for the Rams, was added in 1959. Safety Richie Petitbon was picked up in the 1959 draft and would be a stalwart addition to the defense at safety through the 1968 season. Draft choices and acquisitions added Mike Ditka, Mike Pyle, Roosevelt Taylor, and Dave Whitsell—all picked up in the early 1960s. Taylor who had played for Eddie Robinson at Grambling would not miss a single game in his eight-year career with the Bears.[10]

The improved Bears were ready for another championship run in 1963. The Bears finished the season 11–1–2 to win the Western Conference. In the NFL championship game, the Bears would face Y. A. Tittle's New York Giants. On defense, the Bears featured Bill George, Joe Fortunato, Larry Morris, Doug Atkins, and Ed O'Bradovich. They had beat the defending champion Green Bay Packers of

Vince Lombardi twice that season, 10–3 and 26–7. The Bears had the stingiest defense in the league, whereas the Giants featured a terrific offense.

The Bears would stop Y.A. to win the game. Morris and O'Bradovich each picked off Tittle passes that led to scores. Steady Bill Wade's offense responded by scoring on both opportunities. The Bears beat the Giants 14–10 for their first championship since 1946.

The rest of the 1960s would be a disappointment in the record books as the Bears could not develop a run at the top of the standings. But for Chicago Bear fans it will be remembered for two players who began their careers in 1965 and gave fans a reason to watch each game. On offense, Gale Sayers would light up the league with full out running style featuring impossible cuts that made him incredibly elusive for his short career. In 1965, Sayers would score an incredible 22 touchdowns in his first season, including six in one game against the San Francisco 49ers. Sayers would edge out fellow Bear Dick Butkus, for rookie of the year. Sayers would average 5 yards a carry.

On the defensive side of the ball, Butkus was creating a legacy of toughness by which future Bear defenders would be measured. The Bears would feature many other talented players throughout the decade, but the team would simply fall short of the top echelon.

Prior to the start of the 1968 season, George Halas retired from coaching after 40 seasons with 324 wins, 151 losses, and 31 ties.

Finks Era

The 1970s were about big change for the organization. The Bears played their final season in Wrigley Field in 1970 before moving to Soldier Field. In 1975, the Bears moved their training camp to Lake Forest after spending 31 years at Saint Joseph's College in Rensselaer, Indiana. And tragically, the Bears lost the team president, George "Mugs" Halas, son of Papa Bear, in the final days of the decade on December 16, 1979.

Team founder George Halas would be as busy as ever during his sixth decade of professional football leadership. He was elected president of the National Football Conference as the NFL and AFL merged in 1970. In 1974, Jim Finks joined the Bears as general manager. Finks named Jack Pardee, the first non-Bear in such a position, as head coach.

Walter "Sweetness" Payton was the Bears' first-round draft choice in 1975. He was simply the best football player ever. He could run, block, catch, pass, punt, and kick. There was nothing in football he could not do. He missed one game in his entire pro career and trained with legendary discipline and intensity coming into each training camp in superb condition.

Payton played for 13 seasons with the Chicago Bears, from 1975 to 1987. He rushed 3,838 times for 16,726 yards scoring 110 touchdowns. He rushed over 1,200 yards in a season ten times. He also caught 492 passes for 4,538 yards and 15 more touchdowns. Altogether, he scored 125

JOKING WITH ONE OF THE BEST MEN IN FOOTBALL,
COACH NEILL ARMSTRONG

touchdowns and he accounted for a record 21,803 combined net yards. He gained 100 yards or more from scrimmage in 108 games.

The Bears returned to the playoffs in 1977 under Coach Pardee. Chicago lost in the opening round of the Playoffs to the Dallas Cowboys.

Two years after their last trip to the playoffs, they were back with Coach Neill Armstrong, former defensive coordinator of the Minnesota Vikings. Armstrong posted a 30–34 record while with the Bears and was gone after four seasons, but his tenure created some high spots for the team and its fans. In a gutsy performance on the same day that Mugs Halas died, December 16, 1979, the Bears honored his memory by scorching the Saint Louis Cardinals 42–6 to wipe out a 33 point differential they needed to make the playoffs. On Thanksgiving Day November 27, 1980, the Bears fell behind the Lions 17–3 going into the fourth quarter. After closing the gap to 17–10, quarterback Vince Evans drove the Bears 96 yards down the field with less than four minutes to go to tie the game. The Bears won the overtime coin toss, forcing the Lions to give the ball right back to them. Dave Williams received the kick, ran toward the center of the field, and then cut to side lines and towards the end zone. He covered 95 yards in 21 seconds for the winning score—Bears won 23–17. Another notable victory in the Armstrong era was the Bears massacre of the Packers on December 7, 1980, 61–7.

Ditka Era

The Bears would turn the corner in the 1980s, become a dominant power in the middle of the decade. One of the last big moves made by George Halas was hiring Mike Ditka as head coach in 1982. Papa Bear passed away on October 31, 1983, at the age of 88. His grandson, Michael McCaskey, became president of the Bears.

In 1984, the Bears won the Central Division. They defeated the Washington Redskins to advance to the NFC championship game. That game was a disappointing loss for the Bears, but the 49ers' 23–0 victory was instructive. The Bears' defense had disrupted the play of 49ers legendary quarterback, Joe Montana. The Niners went into the half with two field goals and the Bears had two picks on Montana. But the Bears' offense was not ready for prime time—missing starting quarterback McMahon. The defense wore out and the game proved a motivator for the Bears' next season.

Going into the 1985 season, the Bears looked to improve with the addition of William Perry and Kevin Butler. Perry would prove to be both literally and figuratively a huge boost to the Bears. On defense, he would help to shut down opposing offenses by filling running gaps. On offense, he would occasionally loosen up opposing defensive goal line stands with crushing blocks, power runs, and even the occasional pass pattern. Kicker Butler would prove exceptional—both a steady and a clutch kicker who provided points on the board.

Considered to be one of the finest football teams of all time, the 15–1 Bears were virtually unstoppable in the playoffs, crushing the Giants 21–0, the Rams 24–0, and the New England Patriots 46–10.

In 1986, the Bears were a very strong team that fell short. Quarterback McMahon was a marked man for the year and was injured in the November 23rd game against Green Bay. With McMahon lost for the season, the Bears seemed to recover with Doug Flutie, but lost the divisional playoff game to the Redskins, 27–13.

The Bears had a great core in 1987 and had some brilliant moments. A players' strike marked the season. McMahon recovered from another injury to lead the team at critical junctures. The Bears' 11–4 record was good enough to win their fourth consecutive division title. In the playoffs, the Redskins came back from a 14–0 deficit to beat the Bears 21–17.

In 1988, the Bears were overachievers—taking a team that had lost Walter Payton, Gary Fencik, Wilber Marshall, and Willie Gault to within one game of the Super Bowl. The Bears ended the regular season with a 12–4 mark. They beat the Eagles in a divisional playoff game 20–12 that was remarkable for the dense fog that moved in. After the "Fog Bowl" win, the Bears lost the NFC championship game to the 49ers. After five years of success, the Bears were 6–10 in 1989.

1990s and 2000s

The Bears started the 1990s strong, with a 12–5 mark and the NFC Central title. Jim Harbaugh had a terrific season at quarterback, but was injured when playing Detroit in the 14th game of the season. Mike Tomczak was called in to relieve Harbaugh. The Bears went on to win their first playoff game against the wildcard New Orleans Saints, but lost to the New York Giants, who would become the Super Bowl champions. The 1991 season was an up and down one with several close wins that enabled the Bears to get into the playoffs as a wildcard team. The Bears came up short 17–13 in the wildcard game against Dallas. In 1992, the Bears went 5–11, ending the Ditka era.

Dave Wannstedt took the helm in 1993, and he wheeled and dealed to quickly rebuild the Bears. His rookie 7–5 season was satisfactory for a rebuilding year that saw many changes. The year 1994 saw a stream of veteran Bears including Steve McMichael, Neal Anderson, and Richard Dent leave the club as Wannstedt continued to assemble his team of the future. Another up-and-down season followed, but the 9–7 Bears reached the playoffs. The Bears' quarterback situation was unsettled, with Steve Walsh and Erik Kramer in and out of games. Making the playoffs, the Bears upset the Vikings in their first game, but fell to the powerful 49ers 44–15. Kramer took over as starting quarterback in 1995 and, along with his receivers and running back Rashaan Salaam, the Bears became an offensive powerhouse, but struggled in other areas. However, for 1995, the Bears' 9–7 record was not good enough to make the playoffs. In 1996, the promising Bears went 7–9 in part because of injuries to Erik Kramer, Rashaan Salaam, and Chris Zorich. Nothing worked out for the Bears in 1997 and the team dropped to 4–12. In Wannstedt's last season with the Bears in 1998, they matched their previous 4–12 mark as Erik Kramer fell to injuries again that season.

In 1999, the Bears hired Dick Jauron as head coach and Ted Phillips became president. In the draft, they picked up quarterback Cade McNown from UCLA to run a new offensive scheme to be implemented by new coordinator Gary Crowton. McNown was not ready to move into the starting role that year. Veteran quarterback Shane Matthews played well, but was injured. Jim Miller showed great promise when he came in to backup Matthews. Another troubling season followed in 2000 and the Bears took it on the chin again with a 5–11 finish. McNown got the nod as starting quarterback, but struggled through the first half of the season until a shoulder injury sidelined him. Miller got his opportunity to lead the team, but was also injured. Shane Matthews played well enough down the stretch. On a positive note, linebacker Brian Urlacher was drafted.

In 2001, Mark Hatley, Bears vice-president of player personnel, left the organization and Jerry Angelo was brought in as general manager. Shane Matthews and Jim Miller would swap starting assignments as both were injured, but the season turned out to be one of the most entertaining of all time. The Bear players showed great heart and determination. On October 28, after trailing San Francisco 28–9 in the third quarter, the Bears rallied to tie the game in the last minute and won it in overtime on a Mike Brown interception run for touchdown. The following week, Bears came back from a 21–7 deficit with one minute left against Cleveland. Bears scored, recovered an onside kick, and then scored again in the final seconds. Incredibly, Mike Brown would intercept another pass and run it back for the overtime win. The Bears finished 13–3 and won the Central Division. They lost their first playoff game against Philadelphia, but Chicago was once again excited about the team's prospects for the coming season.

The following 2002 season mark of 4–12 was one the Bears would like to forget. Home games were played at the University of Illinois in Champaign-Urbana as a new Soldier Field was being built. When the Bears started their 2003 season they had a new rookie quarterback, Rex Grossman, but during the season worked in Kordell Stewart and Chris Chandler. The Bears fell short with a final 7–9 record and the Jauron era was over.

In 2004, the Lovie Smith era began. The season mark was a disappointing 5–11 as Smith started to find the right personnel to match his offensive and defensive schemes. Rookie quarterback Kyle Orton stepped in for an injured Rex Grossman in 2005 and led the team toward the playoffs. Grossman returned towards the end of the season to beat the Packers. The Bear defense had a brilliant year. The Bears went on to lose to the Carolina Panthers in the playoffs. In 2006, the Bears had an offense that struggled for several games—but a superb defense. The team came together to win the NFC championship and duke it out with Indianapolis in the Super Bowl. The incomparable Peyton Manning was too much for the Bears, but Thomas Jones had an excellent game. The 29–17 Bear loss capped a successful season. In 2007, the Bears went 7–9, with several injuries to key defensive players. The Bears improved to 9–7 for 2008, with running back Matt Forte having a remarkable year. In 2009, Urlacher's season ended quickly and the defense struggled. Bears acquired the talented Jay Cutler from Denver, but the Bears would fall to 7–9.

Football is an up-and-down game. In the hypercompetitive environment that is the NFL, no team can sustain a top tier position for long. Every team needs to build and then rebuild. The peaks and valleys are part of the process, but we appreciate what has passed and look forward with enthusiasm to what lies ahead. As George Halas, would say, "Who are we playing next week, kid?"

Turning, Turning Myself

On Monday, June 24, 1974, I started working for the Bears fulltime. A couple of years later, the Bears moved from 173 West Madison Street in Chicago to 55 East Jackson

Boulevard, across the street from the historic Old Saint Mary's Church. On Saturdays, my grandfather went to confession at Saint Mary's and he came back to his office to say his penance.

It was a great privilege to work with the energetic and positive George Halas on a day-to-day basis[11]. There were no problems, only opportunities. One morning at the office, I said to my Uncle Mugs (my grandfather's only son) and my father that I had had speaking engagements the last three nights in a row. My grandfather happened to be walking by and overheard the conversation. He asked, "Where are you speaking tonight?"

I replied, "I don't have a speaking engagement tonight."

He said, "That's too bad."

Another day, he called me into his office. He said, "Get a masters degree."

I asked, "Will you pay for it?"

He replied, "Yes."

It was a very short meeting.

I went to DePaul University at night during the off-seasons. He encouraged me with a note: "Long ago I determined that work exceeds talent. Work every day by writing every day. Make me even more proud than I am of you."

His own writing was short and to the point. When he received the Sword of Loyola at the Conrad Hilton, his speech consisted of 55 words:

Reverend Clergy, Mayor Byrne, distinguished award winners, members of the dais, ladies and gentlemen— good evening. Sixty years ago I offered my heart and my helmet to the Lord. My heart is still beating and my helmet still fits. I pray the Divine Coach finds me worthy to be on His first team. Thank you.

Frequently, we ate dinner together after work. When a Bears' fan would stop by our table to ask for an auto- graph, he would always comply. He loved the Bears and appreciated any sign that a fan did, too.

On Thursday, December 10, 1981, George Halas ap- peared before the House Judiciary Committee in Washing- ton, D.C., with Pete Rozelle and Paul Tagliabue. Halas ex- plained how the National Football League was like a wheel. The league was the rim and the teams were the spokes. If you have a weak spoke, you have a weak wheel. That's why the teams with the worst records get to draft first.

That's why the league schedules the games instead of the strong teams just playing each other. That's why the teams share the television money equally.

For family dinners after my grandmother had died, I often drove him out to my parents' home in Des Plaines. He asked me about my girlfriends, and I asked him about his. We had no conflicts because he "never dated anyone under 48."

Each of the last five years of his life, his grandchildren took him out to dinner on his birthday. On February 2,

1983, his 88th birthday, we should have known that something was amiss because he told us that he did not swear anymore. He also said, "May the good Lord grant all of you as long and as wonderful a life as I have had."

On June 26, a special day because it was the anniversary of Grandma Min's birthday, my fiancée, Gretchen Wagle, and I called on Grandpa. He was convalescing and looking frail for the first time in his life. He had purchased the ring I was giving Gretchen over sixty years ago for Grandma Min.

He said, "I bought it for $250 in a pawn shop. I wanted to make sure it was over a carat and yet I wouldn't have paid $750 for it."

He died while I was on the way to Los Angeles to advance the Rams' game. I decided to proceed with the Bears' work the way Grandpa would have wanted. I worked the Rams' press breakfast the next morning and flew to Chicago for the wake and the funeral.

The wake could have been a sad occasion. But so many people came up to my mother and the family to say they were fans and had to come to honor grandpa. Several brought along personal letters from Grandpa or recalled a brief meeting many years before. The wake became a celebration of an extraordinarily rich and full life. Before the casket was closed, my brother Joseph said, "Goodbye, pal."

The funeral was at Saint Ita Church. My brothers Mike, Tim, Ned, Rich, Brian, and I were pallbearers. I read from Lamentations and the Psalms to the congregation, and my brother George read from Paul's Letter to Timothy. In his homily, Father Banet, the president of Saint Joseph's College where the Bears practiced each summer, described George Halas as "a man of faith and a man of prayer."

George Halas was my great friend. He drove hundreds of men to make them the best players and men they could be. At times he could be ruthless in his pursuit of excellence, but he was always relentless in his abiding love of his team. Books are full of stories on how tough he could be. Even the name Bears conjures up an impression of physical abandonment that is in large part his making along with people like Bronko Nagurski, Doug Atkins, Ed Sprinkle, Dick Butkus, Mike Ditka, Mike Singletary, Brian Urlacher, and many others. But there are also many people who have witnessed his quiet acts of kindness over the years. His players were his extended family and he loved them. He never talked about his faith, but those close to him saw evidence of it on a daily basis. Halas was a man of faith, hope, and charity. The Bears of today continue his legacy with tough play on the field and charitable efforts off the field.

LETTER TO BABY

In 1997, Chaz Corzine compiled "a keepsake of blessings and wisdom for new babies" entitled *Letters to Baby.* Broadman & Holman published it. Here is my letter slightly revised for this book.

Dear Baby,

We are three championships behind the Packers. So please don't dawdle too long. We need your help.

We want to win championships with sportsmanship. We do good works quietly, for God's glory. We fear God and we respect our opponents. We are trying to keep the Bears going until The Second Coming. We work diligently and we trust God for the results. Like the Magi who followed the great]star, we go forward in faith.

We are grateful for at least the following: God created a wonderful world in six days; Jesus died for our sins, including fumbles; when we need the Holy Spirit, He is there (He is even there when we think that we don't need Him).

We are hopeful that the world will not end until the Bears have the most championships. Instead of the Super Bowl most valuable player saying that he is going to Disney World, he could say that he is going to heaven. After the presentation of the trophy, the rapture would be a great post game show.

We want to play our games with cooperation that is like an Amish barn-raising. We go to church and Bible study and have daily devotions. Our mandate is to love God and each other. In our attempts to love, we are often funny.

Halas Hall is a place of work and not a den of thieves. It is a halfway house to heaven. Instead of saying, "Please be quiet," we say, "Please become a mime." We give away the credit and we take the blame. We criticize privately and we praise publicly. Instead of singing as soloists, we sing as a chorus. We provide accountability and positive reinforcement for each other.

From William Bennett's book, *The Moral Compass,* we know that "Goethe once said that you must labor to possess what you have inherited. 'If we are not grateful for our gifts and opportunities, we are not likely to value them, and if we do not value them, we are not likely to work hard to preserve and improve them.'"

If you know some people who are not Bear fans, don't be discouraged. Some of the greatest Christians started out as atheists. Jesus forgave the good thief. All they have to do is repent.

Dominus vobiscum,

Patrick McCaskey

— Endnotes —

1   William Emmett Studwell, *The American Song Reader*, (Binghamton, NY: Haworth Press, 1997), 24.

2   Patrick McCaskey with Mike Sandrolini, *Bear with Me, A Family History of George Halas and the Chicago Bears*, (Chicago: Triumph Books, 2009), p. 5.

3   McCaskey with Sandrolini, *Bear with Me, A Family History of George Halas and the Chicago Bears*, 7.

4   Fighting Illini—Official Home of the University of Illinois Athletics, Photo Caption: "Robert Zuppke Helped Lead Illinois to Four of Its Five National Championships," http://www.fightingillini.com (accessed October 27, 2010).

5   McCaskey with Sandrolini, Mike, Bear with Me, 15.

6   McCaskey with Sandrolini, Mike, Bear with Me, 22.

7   McCaskey with Sandrolini, Mike, Bear with Me, 27.

8   McCaskey with Sandrolini, Mike, Bear with Me, 34.

9   McCaskey with Sandrolini, Mike, Bear with Me, 40.

10 Lew Freeman, Lew, *Game of My Life: Chicago Bears: Memorable Stories of Bears Football*, (Champaign: Sports Publishing LLC, 2006) 74.

11 For more reminiscences about George Halas from his grandson, Patrick, see Patrick McCaskey with Mike Sandrolini, *Bear with Me, A Family History of George Halas and the Chicago Bears*, (Chicago: Triumph Books, 2009).

— PHOTOGRAPHS CREDITS —

*All photographs are reproduced with permission
from the sources shown below.*

PAGE	PHOTO DESCRIPTION	SOURCE
Cover and Title Page	Father Freedy	Mark Bolster
viii	Father Freedy	Chaz Palla / *Pittsburgh-Tribune Review*
1	Cabral with U Colorado Players	Cliff Grassmick
18	Bill Wade Throwing	McCaskey Family
28	Bill McCartney on Sidelines	Archives, University of Colorado at Boulder Libraries
29	Baseball Field	David Bernacchi
44	Art Rooney and Steelers in Prayer	AP
45	Byron "Whizzer" White	Archives, University of Colorado at Boulder Libraries
66	Father John Smyth	Tom Connelly/Notre Dame College Prep
74	Pat McCaskey Running	Jonathan Daniel / *Lake County News-Sun* 1981
75	Nancy Swider Peltz	AP
82	Nancy Swider Peltz, Jr.	Steve Penland
90	McCaskey Family	Lee Ann Sanderson
91	Gretchen and Patrick McCaskey	Gil Wagle
101	Walter Payton	AP-Mark Elias
114	Pat McCaskey at Quarterback	*1967 Maridon* / Notre Dame High School Yearbook
115	Brian Piccolo	Archives, Wake Forest University
133	Lombardi at Fordham	Archives and Special Collections, Fordham University Library, Bronx, NY
160	Wally Hilgenberg	AP
161	Monsignor McDermott	Haymarket Center
180	Halas on Sideline	AP-Ernest K. Bennett
181	Halas as Yankee	Library of Congress, Bain Collection
190	Red Grange	Wheaton College, Special Collections
204	McCaskey and Armstrong	Jonathan Daniel / *Lake County News-Sun* 1981